000735

Inequality and Poverty in China in the Age of Globalization

Inequality and Poverty in China in the Age of Globalization

Azizur Rahman Khan
Carl Riskin

OXFORD
UNIVERSITY PRESS
2001

OXFORD
UNIVERSITY PRESS

Oxford   New York

Athens   Auckland   Bangkok   Bogotá   Buenos Aires   Calcutta
Cape Town   Chennai   Dar es Salaam   Delhi   Florence   Hong Kong   Istanbul
Karachi   Kuala Lumpur   Madrid   Melbourne   Mexico City   Mumbai
Nairobi   Paris   São Paulo   Shanghai   Singapore   Taipei   Tokyo   Toronto   Warsaw

and associated companies in

Berlin   Ibadan

Published by Oxford University Press, Inc.
198 Madison Avenue, New York, New York 10016

Oxford is a registered trademark of Oxford University Press

Library of Congress Cataloging-in-Publication Data

Khan, Azizur Rahman.
   Inequality and poverty in China in the age of globalization / Azizur Rahman Kahn,
   Carl Riskin
      p. cm.
   Includes bibliographical references and index.
   ISBN 0-19-513649-7
      1. Poverty—China.   2. Equality—China.   3. Globalization.   I. Khan, Azizur Rhaman.
   II. Title.
HC430.P6 R57 2000
339.5'0951—dc21   00-047906

9 8 7 6 5 4 3 2 1

Printed in the United States of America
on acid-free paper

For

Aubhik Khan
Dibbo Khan
and
Jessica Riskin

with love, affection, and pride

Acknowledgments

We are greatly indebted to Professor Zhao Renwei of the Economics Institute, Chinese Academy of Social Sciences, whose leadership made possible the survey on which this book is based; and to Professor Li Shi, also of the Economics Institute, whose help at every stage of the study contributed immeasurably to its successful completion. Marc Eichen, Stephen J. McGurk, and Jeffrey Zax offered valuable help in designing the survey instruments. We thank Keith Griffin, Rizwanul Islam, Barry Naughton, Samir Radwan, Scott Rozelle, Terry Sicular, James Wen, Zhu Ling, and several anonymous referees who commented on the manuscript of this book and the papers that it is based on.

Acknowledgment is due to the Asian Development Bank and the Ford Foundation for their financial support of the survey and other research expenses. Intramural grants from the Academic Senate of the University of California, Riverside, and financial support from the International Labour Office helped pay for research assistance. Mark Brenner provided computational assistance for much of the empirical work. Zhang Ming helped with many computational problems. We express appreciation for the cooperation of the colleagues at the Chinese Academy of Social Sciences; the participants at the Workshop held in Beijing in August 1997 on the preliminary results of the survey; and the State Statistical Bureau, which implemented the household surveys on which this book is based. The East Asian Institute, Columbia University, provided support facilities as well as a congenial and supportive environment to one of the authors.

Material in Tables 1.2, 2.1, 2.3 to 2.6, and 3.1 to 3.9, and surrounding text, originally appeared in our article, "Income and Inequality in China: Composition, Distribution and Growth of Household Income, 1988 and 1995," in *The China Quarterly*, no. 154, June 1998.

Finally, we express our thanks to Herb Addison, our editor at Oxford University Press, who retired midway through the production of this book, and we wish him a joyful and active life in retirement.

Contents

· ·

1 Introduction, 3

    1. *China's Growth in the Reform Period*, 3
    2. *From Rural Development-Led Growth to Growth Led*
       by Integration with the Global Economy, 4
    3. *Some Features of China's Integration with*
       the Global Economy, 4
    4. *Growth and Distribution*, 7
    5. *Basis for the Present Study*, 8
    6. *Outline of the Study*, 12

2 Household Income: Its Composition and Growth, 14

    1. *Definition of Income and Its Components*, 14
    2. *Income and Its Components: Levels and Changes*, 17
    3. *Difference Between Our Definition and*
       the Official Definition, 22
    4. *Some Implications of the Evidence from the Survey*, 25

3 The Distribution of Income: Evolution of Inequality
  1988–1995, 28

    1. *Introduction*, 28
    2. *Index of Inequality*, 28
    3. *Distribution of Rural Income*, 29
    4. *Distribution of Urban Income*, 35
    5. *Overall Distribution of Income in China*, 40

6. *Regional Inequality*, 44
7. *Summary of Findings*, 49

4 Trends in the Incidence of Poverty, 52

1. *Introduction*, 52
2. *Estimating Poverty Thresholds*, 57
3. *Estimates of Poverty*, 64
4. *A Summary of Findings and a Comparison with Others' Results*, 75
    Appendix: Deriving the Poverty Thresholds, 78

5 Gender, Health and Education: Human Development Dimensions of Inequality, 81

1. *Introduction: The Human Development Index*, 81
2. *Human Development*, 82
3. *Gender Inequality*, 85
4. *Problems in the Distribution of Health Care*, 95
    Appendix: Human Development Index by Province in 1995, 102

6 Explaining the Increase in Inequality and the Decline in Poverty Reduction, 103

1. *Introduction*, 103
2. *Gap Between Growth in GDP and Growth in Personal Income*, 104
3. *Sources of Increased Inequality in Income Distribution*, 107
4. *Growth, Inequality, and Poverty*, 117
5. *Conclusion*, 120

7 Policies for the Reduction of Inequality and Poverty, 121

1. *Introduction*, 121
2. *Need for a Comprehensive Strategy*, 124
3. *Reduction of Urban/Rural Gap and Policies for the Rural Economy*, 125
4. *Regional Balance in Development*, 128
5. *Reversing the Disequalizing Effect of the Fiscal System and Transfer Payments*, 129
6. *Urban Employment*, 135
7. *Migration Policies*, 137

8. *Targeted Support to the Poor,* 139

9. *Macroeconomic Policies and Implications,* 140

10. *Implications for Globalization,* 141

11. *Conclusion,* 142

8 Summary and Conclusions, 143

1. *Income Composition and Distribution,* 144

2. *Poverty,* 146

3. *Human Development and Inequality,* 148

4. *Explanations,* 151

5. *Implications for Policy,* 154

Notes, 159

Bibliography, 175

Index, 181

Inequality and Poverty in China in the Age of Globalization

1

Introduction

· ·

1. China's Growth in the Reform Period

China's development since the period of transition to a market economy began in 1979 has had a number of remarkable features. The most obvious of these is the astonishingly rapid rate of economic growth that followed the introduction of reforms. The average annual rate of growth of GDP was 10.2% during the 1980s and 12.8% during the first half of the 1990s, as compared to 5.5% during the 1970s.[1] During the period from the beginning of reforms to the terminal year covered by the present study—i.e., between 1979 and 1995—China's annual rate of population growth was just under 1.4%. Thus, per capita GDP almost quadrupled over this period. Never before in the course of human history has a quadrupling of per capita GDP of more than one-fifth of humankind occurred over such a short period.

This unprecedented pace of growth coincided with a remarkable stability in the rate of growth. Through tumultuous reform of basic social institutions and a rapid integration with the global economy, China has avoided negative growth in every year since reforms began. This is in sharp contrast to the performance of the world's other former centrally planned economies, which invariably experienced years of negative growth while reforming their economic systems. At the time of writing, more than a year after several countries renowned for having staged the Asian miracle were plunged into a deep crisis, China—though clearly touched by the Asian crisis—has suffered much milder effects.

2. From Rural Development-Led Growth to Growth Led by Integration with the Global Economy

The period of China's uninterrupted hyper-growth since the beginning of reforms can be divided into two distinct subperiods which represent very different strategies of growth. Prior to the mid-1980s, China's growth and reform were focused principally on agriculture and the rural economy. The reform program began in agriculture with a complete change in the system of ownership and incentives, and a sharp improvement in agriculture's terms of trade, brought about by a rise in procurement prices. The result was all-round development of the rural economy, the effects of which spilled over to the rest of the economy. The ratio of urban to rural per capita personal income fell from 2.37 in 1978 to 1.70 in 1983.[2] From about the middle of the 1980s, the rate of growth of agricultural output slowed, partly as a result of the public policy of halting—and, for a period, reversing—the improvement of agriculture's terms of trade, and partly from a decline in public expenditure for agriculture. The growth in the rest of the rural economy could not offset these trends. The ratio of urban to rural per capita personal income started rising sharply after 1985 and reached as high as 2.6 by 1994, according to official estimates.[3] After 1994 the ratio declined somewhat, though it still remained well above the bottom to which it had fallen in 1983.[4]

Growth in the period since the mid-1980s was led by exports fostered by a strategy of greater integration with the globalizing world economy. During this period, the rate of export growth far exceeded that of other components of GDP, and a number of changes in international economic relations brought about a fundamental reorientation in the pattern of China's growth.

3. Some Features of China's Integration with the Global Economy

Some indicators of these changes are shown in Table 1.1. Although China's exports, as a proportion of GDP, changed little between 1980 (10.1%) and 1985 (10.5%), they grew rapidly thereafter and reached 21.2% of GDP in 1995. The composition of exports also began to change dramatically from about the middle of the 1980s. Primary goods accounted for more than half of China's merchandise exports in 1980, and there was little change in their share by 1985. Thereafter, however, the share of primary goods fell sharply. Manufactured exports, as a proportion of total exports, rose from 49.4% in 1985 to 85.6%

TABLE 1.1. Some Indicators of China's Integration with the Global Economy

	Exports as Percentage of GDP	Manufactured Exports as Percentage of Merchandise Exports	Foreign Direct Investment (Billion $)	External Debt (Billion $)
1980	10.1	49.7	0.06	4.50
1985	10.5	49.4	1.03	16.70
1990	19.1	74.4	3.49	52.63
1995	21.2	85.6	35.85	118.10

Note: Exports in column 1 refer to exports of goods and non-factor services. The second column is based on the data in SSB, 1997. All the other estimates are based on the data in World Bank 1995a and World Bank 1997f.

in 1995. Until the middle of the 1980s China received very little foreign capital inflow, but it has since become a major recipient of foreign capital, principally in the form of foreign direct investment (FDI). In 1995 China absorbed $35.9 billion of FDI—38% of the total FDI received by all low- and middle-income countries of the world.)

China's external indebtedness increased during this period, although its debt burden remained low by international standards. The debt to GNP ratio at the end of 1996 stood at 20%, less than half the average for developing countries and among the lowest such ratios in Asia.[5] Total debt service, as a proportion of exports of goods and services, was only 9.9% (as compared to 27.9% for India, 15.4% for all low-income countries, and 17.4% for all middle-income countries).[6]

During this period, China substantially liberalized its foreign trade regime. Although this claim must be qualified because of the continued existence of non-tariff barriers, tariff rates have fallen drastically. Estimates are available only for the 1990s; they indicate that the weighted mean tariff on all products fell from 40.6% in 1992 to 25.4% in 1996, and 20.9% in 1997.[7] China's integration with the global economy, however, has avoided liberalizing the capital account, a policy that has kept China immune to the kind of financial crisis that hit several Asian countries in the second half of 1997.

The reasons behind the change in the development strategy—beyond general tributes to the value of "opening up" and the benefits of "letting some get rich first"—have not been officially discussed and are not entirely clear. Two possible explanations, however, suggest themselves. China's initial reform program, with its emphasis on improving agriculture's terms of trade, imposed a heavy burden on the state budget and contributed to reducing the rate of overall savings from 34.1% of GDP in 1978 to 27.9% in 1981. Improved efficiency of resource use made it possible for the growth rate to accelerate over this period, but the government must have been concerned about the financial consequences of its agricultural policies, which were substantially revised. Second, by the mid-1980s China must have been convinced that its ability to maintain rapid growth over the long-term future called for a source of growth other than agriculture, and the globalizing world economy presented it with a clear opportunity that needed to be grasped.[8]

Economic theory argues that trade liberalization and increased integration with the global economy contribute both to efficiency and to equity. Greater efficiency is brought about by the restructuring of production in accordance with comparative advantage, the discipline of external competition, and the inflow of capital and technology. A restructuring of production more in accordance with comparative advantage leads to a greater use of the abundant factor of production, which in China's case is labor. This should increase employment and wages and lead to an improvement in income distribution and a reduction in poverty.

There is little reason to doubt that integration with the global economy has led to increased economic efficiency in China. It is, however, possible to argue that economic theory's prediction of the distributional outcome of integration completely abstracts from specific initial conditions. It is easy to see how the process of integration might contribute to increased inequality and weaken the impetus for poverty reduction in the specific circumstances of China. As we have seen, growth of exports greatly exceeded that of the other components of demand. Export production, in turn, was concentrated in the rich provinces of the eastern coastal region. Coastal provinces, with easy access to ports and more developed infrastructure than the rest of the country, also received a disproportionately high share of FDI, which was a source of more advanced technology and higher productivity. This disequalizing trend was exacerbated by government policies such as the location of "special economic zones" and open cities with differentially favorable conditions for FDI in coastal areas; this discouraged any inclination foreign investors might have had to explore the more backward interior of the country.

Although there were a number of reasons for the decision to launch a serious reform of state and collective enterprises in the late 1990s, one of these reasons was surely to attract more FDI into collaborative relationships. While promoting greater productive efficiency, these reforms also led to a loss of social protection for workers who were laid off when government declined to cover losses of state enterprises and sought to make them lean and market-oriented. This is an outcome that is due specifically to the heavy reliance of China's social protection policy in the past on making state and collective enterprises absorb far more labor than they needed.

Despite the large inflow of FDI and foreign capital, the pressure on domestic saving was not eased. Paradoxically, the period of rapid inflow of FDI has witnessed a consistently higher rate of saving than of investment.[9] Much of this apparent paradox appears to be due to the meteoric increase in the volume of international reserves that China has accumulated over the past decade, from $13.2 billion in 1985 to $80.3 billion in 1995.[10] Thus, the liberalization of capital inflow and the friendliness to FDI in the period of globalization have not meant a reduction in the drive—characteristic of the pre-reform Chinese economy—for an ever-increasing rate of domestic saving.[11] Rising saving rates, in turn, kept the rate of growth in personal income substantially below that of GDP. Since it is personal income growth that is the principal determinant of living standard for the purposes of estimating poverty, the rate of poverty reduction was smaller than it would have been if growth of personal income had kept up with that of GDP.

Although China's integration with the global economy per se is not the subject of this study, one of our arguments is that trends in China's income distribution and poverty in the period under review were strongly influenced by, among other things, policies related to this integration. We argue that certain features of globalization, in the absence of compensatory public action, exacerbated the tendency toward increased inequality in the distribution of income.

4. Growth and Distribution

China's reform program began with a clear anticipation that income distribution would become less egalitarian. The authors of the program argued that the promotion of extreme and artificial income equality in the pre-reform period negated economic incentives and efficiency and thereby constituted a drag on the rate of economic growth. Pre-reform policies that promoted equality—prohibition of virtually all forms of private enterprise, divorce of the distribution of earnings from the distribution of productivity, and guaranteed employment for life—were scornfully referred to by reformers as the "iron rice bowl" and "everyone eating from the same big pot."

Reforms were focused on abolishing past policies of inefficient egalitarianism with the intention of simultaneously promoting a higher growth in output and a greater differentiation in earnings. The authors of China's economic reform, however, expected that virtually everyone would gain from growth, so that any increase in inequality would be accompanied by a reduction in poverty—i.e., a decline in the proportion of population below some absolute level of income representing a minimum acceptable standard of living. The official view was that "a rising tide lifts all boats," and the expectation was clearly that the increase in inequality would not be great enough to outweigh the effect of higher growth and thus to induce greater poverty.

Early evidence seemed to indicate that these expectations were indeed realized. World Bank estimates, based on the official data reported by the household surveys carried out by the State Statistical Bureau (SSB), showed that in the early years after the institution of reforms, inequality in distribution of income actually declined for a period before beginning to rise in the early 1980s. The incidence of poverty also declined rather dramatically.[12]

From about the middle of the 1980s—the beginning of the shift in China's development focus away from the rural economy and toward integration with the global economy—China experienced increasingly more disequalizing and less poverty-alleviating growth. Estimates based on official data suggested an increase in inequality of the distribution of income and a sharp decline in the rate of poverty reduction.[13]

5. Basis for the Present Study

There was a great deal of interest among the development community in understanding these trends, but there was also a strong feeling that these momentous findings were based on a fragile statistical foundation. Dissatisfaction with the estimates of inequality and poverty in China, based on official data, was widespread, in part because the SSB's definition of household income was unsatisfactory. For example, it did not include the rental value of owned housing, and its accounting of income in kind and income transfers was at best partial. Moreover, the SSB data were reported in too highly aggregated a form to permit a careful analysis of income distribution and poverty.

Since the beginning of reforms, a great deal of effort has been directed to the estimation of indices of inequality and poverty in China. Most of the research on these estimates had to be carried out within the above-mentioned limitations of the official data on income distribution. From a methodological standpoint, this research can be classified into three main categories. First, there are studies that have accepted the limitations of the official data. Most of the research on China's inequality and poverty at the national level—e.g., various

World Bank studies and the official Chinese estimates referred to in the subsequent chapters—fall in this category. Their results have to be qualified because of the limitations of the official distributional data. A second group of studies tried to make adjustments for various inadequacies of the official data. These have invariably been limited to selected regions or provinces for which information needed to make advances over officially published data was available. Ravallion and Chen (1998) and Jalan and Ravallion (1998), which exploited access to data sets produced by the State Statistical Bureau's full rural household income surveys for several contiguous southern provinces over several years, are examples of this kind of work. These researchers are able to make adjustments for specific omissions and inadequacies in the official survey data for the particular provinces for which information was available, but this is possible for only some of the inadequacies and a few provinces. Although this work has provided highly useful insights on specific issues,[14] the limitations of its scope prevent it from supplying a comprehensive correction of the official procedures followed in the household surveys as a whole. Finally, some studies have tried to generate new data of their own for very small areas. Lyons (1994) is an example. Again, this work sheds extremely useful light on the process of growth and distribution, but it is not a substitute for reliable estimates of inequality and its change over time in China as a whole.

A major research project was implemented in the late 1980s by an international group of economists in collaboration with the Institute of Economics of the Chinese Academy of Social Sciences to provide better data on income distribution. The first comprehensive effort to estimate household income and its distribution in China according to standard international definitions was made by implementing a household survey for 1988 as the reference year.[15] The sample for the survey was a subsample drawn from the SSB panel for household surveys.[16] The results of the survey demonstrated that the estimates of household income based on the annual surveys of the State Statistical Bureau (SSB) were inadequate both as indicators of living standard and as a source for the estimation of the degree of inequality of income distribution. The study showed that per capita household income was much higher and more unequally distributed than suggested by the SSB estimates. It also provided useful insights into the sources of inequality in China which were unobtainable from the highly aggregated reporting of official estimates of income and its distribution.

The 1988 survey greatly expanded our knowledge about the level, composition, and distribution of China's income. After a few years, however, its authors and many of its users came to feel that a repetition of the survey was urgently needed in order to understand how China's income and its distribution had changed since 1988. Whereas the 1988 study provided a single snapshot of China's income structure, a second survey would yield insights about how this structure was changing over time in response to remarkable growth and equally remarkable changes in economic institutions, attitudes, and policies.

The survey was therefore repeated for 1995 as the reference year. Table 1.2 summarizes some features of the surveys of 1988 and 1995. The main difference between the two surveys is the reduction in coverage in 1995. The rural sample was close to 12% of the SSB parent sample of 67,340 households in 1995. Although a larger sample size would have been desirable, the decision in this regard was largely dictated by the tradeoff between enlarging the sample size and incorporating the details required for a comprehensive and accurate measurement of income and related variables, given our limited resources. For rural China as a whole, the sample size in 1995 by itself does not create a serious problem of comparison with previous results, although the sample size at the provincial level may have become too small to avoid an unacceptably large sampling error for certain measurements.

TABLE 1.2. Comparison of the Surveys for 1988 and 1995

	1988	1995
Rural Sample		
Number of households	10,258	7,998
Number of persons	51,352	34,739
Average household size	5.006	4.343
Number of provinces included in the survey	28	19
Provinces included in 1988 but excluded in 1995	Heilongjiang, Inner Mongolia, Qinghai, Ningxia, Guangxi, Fujian, Hainan, Tianjin, Shanghai	
Urban Sample		
Number of households	9,009	6,931
Number of persons	31,827	21,694
Average household size	3.533	3.131
Number of provinces included in survey	10	11
Provinces included in 1995 but not in 1988		Sichuan

The other important difference between the two surveys is the smaller number of rural provinces covered in 1995. In 1988, only two provinces—Tibet and Xinjiang—were excluded from the rural sample; in 1995, nine others were excluded (see Table 1.2). Care was exercised in choosing the provinces for exclusion from the rural sample. These are uniformly spread among the provinces in terms of their ranking according to per capita rural income. The average rank of the excluded provinces for 1988 was 14.9 out of a total of 28 provinces. It is therefore reasonable to hope that the reduction in number of provinces covered in the rural sample does not create a significant bias.

Our urban sample in 1995 was 19% of the parent SSB sample of 36,370 drawn nationally from 226 cities and counties. Urban locations were selected to represent urban entities in different regions of China and cities and towns of different size. In 1995, there was an addition of one province, Sichuan, to the urban sample. Nevertheless, the restricted number of provinces covered by the urban sample is a source of concern, especially given the differentiation in urban economic activity in recent years.

The most serious problem with the SSB sample is that its urban panel excludes the "floating population," those who have migrated for extended periods of time to urban areas but have not been granted urban residence permits (hukou).[17] Because they were excluded from the official household survey samples drawn by the SSB, these migrants were necessarily excluded from our subsamples as well. They are reported to have numbered about 72 million—one-fifth of the registered urban population—according to a Labor Ministry Survey for 1995.

It is impossible to determine how the exclusion of the migrants has affected the results of the survey. By all available accounts, the migrants have an average income which is lower than that of the official urban population. It is therefore virtually certain that our estimates of urban income are higher than they would have been if the migrants had been included; however, it is also certain that the average income of these migrants is higher than the average income of the rural population. Thus, it is impossible to know how the exclusion of the migrants would affect the estimate of average household income for all Chinese households from the results of the survey. Nor do we know how excluding the migrants has affected the estimate of the growth rate for average household income of all urban households: it is possible that the rate of growth of migrants' household income has differed from that of the income of official residents, but there is no way to tell which of these two rates was higher. Given the lower average income of migrants, it is virtually certain that their inclusion would have led to a higher estimate of the proportion of the urban population below a given poverty threshold. But it is not possible to argue that their inclusion would have given a higher estimate of inequality as measured by standard indices like the Gini ratio. The fact that their average income is lower than the average income of the official residents by itself does not tell us anything about the effect of their inclusion on inequality, in the absence of information on how their incomes are distributed.

6. Outline of the Study

In the next chapter, we are concerned with estimating urban and rural household incomes and their distributions among different sources. Chapter 2 also examines the changes in these estimates between 1988 and 1995 and compares them with their official counterparts—a comparison that raises important questions concerning the accuracy of China's official macroeconomic accounts.

Chapter 3 makes separate estimates of inequality and the contribution of different sources of income to inequality for the rural and urban sectors, and for China as a whole. It also compares the degree and sources of inequality in 1988 and 1995 and identifies the main factors contributing to increasing inequality between the two years.

Chapter 4 derives alternative absolute poverty thresholds for 1988 and 1995 and uses them to estimate various indices of poverty in rural and urban China for those two years, and thus to assess the change over time in the incidence of poverty according to different indices.

Chapter 5 explores the dimensions of inequality and poverty other than income. It looks at the distribution of access to social services like education and health and also considers the issue of gender inequality.

Chapter 6 tries to explain the increase in inequality and the decline in the rate of poverty reduction between 1988 and 1995, a period of extraordinarily rapid growth of China's economy. In particular, it relates the disequalizing pattern of growth during this period to the specific development strategy adopted by China since the middle of the 1980s.

Chapter 7 discusses the policies that China needs to consider in order to arrest the disequalizing trends that have characterized its growth in the recent past. Chapter 8 concludes the study with a comprehensive summary of its main arguments and findings.

Throughout the book, we present the results of the 1995 survey in detail. Since the 1988 survey results have been available for several years, they are discussed here chiefly in the context of comparisons with 1995. Readers who want to know more about the 1988 survey itself are referred to the existing literature.[18]

2

Household Income: Its Composition and Growth

· ·

1. Definition of Income and Its Components

The household is the basic unit of estimation in this study. Household income includes the earnings of each individual member as well as the collective earnings of the household from enterprises, property, and transfer. Each member of a household is assumed to have the same income, the per capita income of the household. As have other studies of this kind, we have found it impossible to address the issue of intra-household difference in income.

Components of Rural Income

We have used the same definition of income as in 1988, except that, owing to changes in economic and social policies, certain components of income have become extinct since 1988. For rural China the components of income are as follows:

1.   Income from wages, pensions, and other forms of labor compensation accruing to individual members of the household. In addition to cash earnings, all income in kind, valued at market prices, has been included.
2.   Income, other than compensation for labor, accruing to individual members from private and joint venture enterprises, plus income from collective welfare funds. This category is distinct from income accruing from enterprises *owned by the household*.
3.   Net income from farming. This includes the value of all

output of agricultural, forestry, and fishery products, either sales or household consumption valued at market price, net of all costs of purchased inputs, including non-household labor.

4. Net income from non-farm enterprises and subsidiary activities. This includes the output of all non-farm activities less the cost of purchased inputs including non-household labor. It should be noted that, for 1988, it was not possible to distinguish net farm income from net income from non-farm activities. Instead, we had net cash income from the sale of all farm and non-farm activities, and gross value of consumption of farm products; together, these two items added up to what in 1995 is the sum of net income from farming and non-farm activities. For purposes of comparison with 1988, we have estimated the gross value of consumption of farm products, although it is no longer a separate component of income according to the classification adopted in 1995.

5. Income from property. This consists of interest on savings deposits and bonds, dividends, and rent on leased-out land, house, and other property.

6. Rental value of owned housing. Only the rental value of the owned part of the house occupied is included. As in 1988, it is assumed to be 8% of the difference between the replacement value of the house and the debt on the house.[1] Replacement value is estimated by applying the provincial average replacement cost per square meter of rural housing to the size of the house in square meters. Thus, our estimated inequality in the distribution of rental value of owned housing necessarily reflects the inequality in (indirectly estimated) housing assets (which, for rural China, turns out to be quite small).

7. Net transfer from the state, local government and the remnants of the old collectives. This includes all welfare and relief payments and subsidies received by the household, less all taxes and compulsory payments to the state and the collectives.

8. Other income. This residual category is dominated by remittances made by migrant members of the household working elsewhere, and it also includes gifts received from private donors and miscellaneous sources of income not classified elsewhere.

Components of Urban Income

Sources of urban income in 1995 are fewer than in 1988. Two components of 1988 classification—income of nonworking members and ration coupon subsidies—have been eliminated by institutional changes and the abolition of urban food rationing. The remaining components of urban income are as follows:

1. Cash labor compensation of all working members of the household. This includes wages, bonuses, overtime payments, subsidies, and special cash payments from primary and secondary jobs. Wages are here defined to include allowances received by workers furloughed from enterprises that are downsizing employment—a growing phenomenon as the reform of state enterprises proceeds.
2. Income of retired members. This includes both pensions and post-retirement jobs.
3. Income from private and individual enterprises owned/operated by the household.
4. Income from property. This includes the same items as rural property income.
5. Housing subsidy in kind. This component consists of the difference between market rent (directly estimated by the head of each household surveyed) and the actual rent paid by all those who are occupying public housing.[2]
6. Other net subsidies. This includes all subsidies and payments in kind, other than housing subsidy, including in-kind compensation for labor. It also includes relief payments and hardship subsidies. All direct taxes and fees have been subtracted.
7. Rental value of owner-occupied housing. For households living in their own houses, the market rent (directly estimated by the household heads) has been included. Estimated interest on housing debt has been subtracted from the estimated rental value of housing.
8. Other income. This consists of private transfers and other minor sources of income not classified under other headings.

2. Income and Its Components: Levels and Changes

Rural Income

Table 2.1 summarizes the level and composition of rural income in 1995. It also shows the composition of rural income in 1988 according to our survey and the annually compounded real rates of growth between 1988 and 1995. The last are based on point comparisons, as are all subsequent estimates of change in variables estimated from the two surveys.

Household production activities (components 3 and 4) remain the single largest source of income, although their share of total income fell from 74% in 1988 to 56% in 1995. Income from farm production accounts for an overwhelming proportion of income from these sources. This too, however, appears to have fallen as a proportion of total income between 1988 and 1995.[3]

Wages are the second largest component of rural income. Their share increased sharply, from about 9% of the total in 1988 to over 22% in 1995. The rise in the share of wages accounts for about three-quarters of the fall in the share of household production in income.

TABLE 2.1. Per Capita Disposable Rural Income (Values in Yuan Per Year)

Income and Its Sources	1995 Amount	1995 Percent	1988 Percent	Real Growth Rate
Total	2306.63	100.00	100.00	4.71
1. Individual wages etc.	516.78	22.38	8.73	19.78
2. Receipts from enterprises	139.89	6.06	2.40	19.49
3. Net farm income	1072.15	46.44 }		
4. Net income from non-farm activities	224.08	9.71 }	74.21	0.62
5. Income from property	9.98	0.43	0.17	19.41
6. Rental value of owned housing	267.93	11.61	9.67	7.48
7. Net transfer from state & collective	−10.99	−0.48	−1.90	−14.07
8. Other income (private transfer etc.)	88.81	3.85	6.71	−3.29
Memo item:				
Gross value of self-consumption of food	659.37	28.66	41.13	−0.61

Note: Real growth rate is estimated by deflating the 1995 estimate by the overall rural CPI—not the price index of the component—and estimating the annual compound rate of growth between 1988 (for which the value from the 1988 survey is used) and 1995.

Rental value of owner-occupied housing is the next important source of income. This increased moderately, from close to 10% of total income to close to 12%.

"Receipts from enterprises" is a category whose components may have changed between 1988 and 1995. In the latter year, it appears to be dominated by income from entrepreneurial activities. If this is combined with net income from household non-farm activities, the sum comes to about 16% of total income, which is one way of assessing the relative importance of private entrepreneurial activity in the rural economy. "Entrepreneurial income" included in "receipts from enterprises" differs from "net income from household non-farm activities" in that the former arises from activity of individuals and the latter from household operations. While in practice the borderline may be somewhat blurred — e.g., some respondents might have regarded a particular activity as individual, others as a family operation — the survey took care to avoid duplication of the reporting of the data in both the categories.

The remaining sources of income are each very small. Income from property has increased at a much faster rate than total income, but it remains minuscule as a proportion of total income. Reported property income is a small fraction of that implied by data on bank savings deposits and relevant interest rates. Yet our estimate appears to be consistent with that of SSB (SSB lumps property income from its household survey together with transfers; the combined estimate is virtually identical to ours). Whether or not the data on bank deposits from alternative sources show that both SSB and we have missed a part of this income is an issue on which we would like to reserve judgment, given the ambiguity of the evidence. For instance, it is apparently not uncommon for enterprises to place their funds in individual accounts, which bear higher interest rates. Nor is it certain that reported official interest rates are applicable to all deposits, especially those held by local savings institutions.

"Miscellaneous" sources of income, dominated by private transfer, have fallen sharply as a proportion of total income. There was also a sharp reduction in the average rate of *net* taxes (i.e., taxes and compulsory payments to the state and collective less subsidies received from them) on rural households (component 7), although taxes still outweigh subsidies for an average household.

Real rates of growth have been estimated by deflating 1995 income and its components by the rural consumer price index (CPI) of the SSB. This is a Paasche index with 1985 as the base. The "Rural CPI" (in Table 2.2, which also shows a number of other indicators of price changes in China) is actually the value of SSB's rural CPI for

TABLE 2.2. Indicators of Price Changes
(Indices for 1995 with 1988 = 100)

Rural CPI	220.09
Urban CPI	227.90
Industrial consumers' price index	206.86
Industrial producers' price Index	238.42
Industrial products rural retail price index	198.27
Grain purchase price	257.75
Overall farm products purchase price	215.91
GNP deflator	204.40
Urban grain purchasers' price	489.09
Unit cost of a kcalorie: rural	299.00
Unit cost of a kcalorie: urban	394.60

Note: All but the last three items are based on SSB data reported in SSB (1996). The last three items are estimated from SSB survey data reported in SSB (1989, 1996). Unit cost of a kcalorie is estimated from a selection of items of food consumption for which information is available for both 1988 and 1995. For urban China, this refers to the composition of food for the low-income group (the poorest two deciles).

1995 as percent of the same for 1988. It is rather unusual for the CPIs to be based on the Paasche formula, which is known to understate the rate of increase in cost of living.[4] In this case, however, the use of the Paasche formula makes it impossible even to interpret the "index" showing the change in CPI between 1988 and 1995.[5]

That the changes in rural and urban CPIs between 1988 and 1995 understate the increase in consumer prices is very strongly suggested by the other indicators of price change shown in Table 2.2. Thus, the unit costs of a kilocalorie of food energy increased at very high rates. If they were combined with the lowest of the indices showing the change in the cost of non-food goods, the resulting CPIs would be far greater; however, we accept the "change" in the official CPI as the deflator, recognizing that this may result in an overestimation of the growth rate.

Of the components of income, wages had the most rapid rate of growth, closely followed by receipts from enterprises and property income. Rental value of owner-occupied housing also had a much higher than average rate of growth. Net income from production activities had a very slow rate of growth. Gross value of self-consumption, a component of net income from production activities, had a negative real growth rate.

It is worth noting that the composition of rural income has changed in favor of the disequalizing components.[6] In 1988, wages were the most disequalizing component of income, indicating a high degree of inequality of access to this source of income. Self-consumption of farm products was the most equalizing component of income. If the inequality of distribution of each component of rural income remained exactly the same as in 1988, the Gini ratio of rural income distribution would rise from its 1988 value of 0.338 to 0.405 in 1995 simply because of the change in the composition of income.[7]

Urban Income

Table 2.3 summarizes information about the level and composition of urban income in 1995. It also shows the composition of urban income according to the 1988 survey and the real growth rates between 1988 and 1995.[8]

Cash wages are by far the largest component of income, contributing more than three-fifths of household income, compared to 44% in 1988. Income of retired members—pensions and earnings from reemployment—is a distant runner-up, contributing just under 12% of income, up from under 7% in 1988.

Rental value of owner-occupied housing, the next largest component, has grown sharply, from less than 4% of income in 1988 to more than 11%. Together with the subsidy on public housing, it accounts for roughly the same proportion of income in 1995 (21%) as in 1988

TABLE 2.3. Per Capita Disposable Urban Income (Values in Yuan Per Year)

Income and Its Sources	1995 Amount	1995 Percent	1988 Percent	Real Growth Rate
Total	5706.19	100.00	100.00	4.48
1. Cash income of working members (wages, etc.)	3497.77	61.30	44.42	17.32
2. Income of retired members (pensions, etc.)	667.14	11.69	6.83	12.83
3. Private/individual enterprises owned	30.23	0.53	0.74	−0.31
4. Income from property	72.28	1.27	0.49	19.60
5. Housing subsidy in kind	555.66	9.74	18.14	−4.40
6. Other net subsidies	71.12	1.25	20.94	−69.82
7. Rental value of owner-occupied housing	650.12	11.39	3.90	21.78
8. Other income	161.87	2.84	4.53	−2.30

Note: Other net subsidies in 1988 include ration coupon subsidies, which were abolished prior to 1995. Real growth rates, in percent per year between 1988 and 1995, are estimated in the same way as in rural China.

(22%). Total "expenditure" on housing requires the further addition of actual rent paid on rented accommodation, which was 0.7% of income in 1988 and 2.8% of income in 1995.[9] Thus, the total "expenditure" on housing was marginally higher as a proportion of income in 1995 (23.8%) than in 1988 (22.7%).

However, the distribution of the housing cost burden changed dramatically. In 1988, 80% of cost was borne by public subsidy, 17% by owner-occupiers, and only 3% by renters. By 1995, the share of total cost borne by public subsidy had fallen by half, to 41%; the share borne by owner-occupiers had almost trebled to 48%; and renters' share had quadrupled to almost 12%.

The sharp fall in housing subsidies was exceeded by that of non-housing subsidies, which dropped from 21% of urban income in 1988 to a negligible 1.25% in 1995. Income from property increased as a proportion of income, though remaining a very small proportion of it. Other sources of income, mainly transfers, fell quite sharply as a proportion of income.

Growth rates in urban real income and its components have been estimated in the same way as the growth rates in rural real income, by deflating 1995 incomes by the change in the urban CPI shown in Table 2.2. The highest annual rate of growth between 1988 and 1995 was in rental value of owned housing. This is due not just to increased rents but more particularly to the pace of housing reform, which has strongly encouraged urban renters to purchase their own apartments. Our results suggest that this reform has made very substantial progress: in 1988 only 13.8% of our urban sample reported living in their own private housing, whereas in 1995 this proportion had risen to 41.7%.

The second fastest growing component was property income, which, however, still amounted to only a little more than 1% of total income. Cash wages was the next most rapidly growing component, increasing at an average annual rate of 17%; it was followed by the earnings of retirees, growing by almost 13%. The growth of retirement income reflects the rapid aging of the Chinese population. In 1988, only 8.4% of the urban sample reported being retired, whereas by 1995 the retired fraction had grown to 13.7%.

The remaining components of urban income had negative real rates of growth. The most remarkable decline occurred in net subsidies (subsidies less taxes), which, as pointed out above, fell from over one-fifth of total income to only 1%.

Unlike the case of rural China, the change in composition of income in urban China does not indicate an a priori direction of change in the distribution of income. On the evidence of the distribution in

1988, wages—the largest source of urban income, and one of the most rapidly growing—is an equalizing component of urban income. On the other hand, the other rapidly growing sources—the rental value of owned housing and income of retirees—are disequalizing components. With the distribution of individual components of urban income remaining the same as in 1988, the composition of income in 1995 would have left the overall inequality of the distribution of urban income virtually unchanged.[10] Thus, any increase in urban inequality must be explained with reference to increasing inequality of the distribution of individual components of income, not by the change in the composition of income itself.

3. Difference Between Our Definition and the Official Definition

The difference between the definition of income adopted by this study and the definition that is employed by the SSB, in the published income estimates for urban and rural households, can be gauged only in broad terms and appears to have remained unchanged since 1988. The SSB excludes rental value of owner-occupied housing. Its coverage of income in kind and subsidies is much less comprehensive than ours. It also appears to catch fewer items of income from household production activities.

Several of the components excluded by the SSB have been changing rapidly as a proportion of total income. This has led to a serious bias in the rate of growth of household income estimated from the official data. Furthermore, the change in the proportion of the excluded components to total income is quite different between rural and urban China. As a consequence, the trend in the rural-urban disparity in income, as estimated from the official data, is also quite misleading.

Rural Income

The real rate of increase in per capita rural income—4.71% per year—is higher than the rate obtained from the SSB estimates (which, using the same deflator as above, turns out to be 4% per year). This suggests that the extent of underestimation of rural income by the SSB is greater for 1995 than for 1988. Per capita rural income estimated from our survey was 46% higher than the SSB estimate in 1995, compared to 39% higher in 1988. This is mainly because the SSB does not count some of the rapidly growing components of income, such as the rental value of owner-occupied housing.

As in 1988, the SSB underestimated all the major components of income (Table 2.4). The largest part—37% of the difference between our estimate and that of the SSB—is explained by the SSB's neglect of the rental value of owner-occupied housing. Their lower estimate of "laborers' remuneration" (*laodongzhe shouru*)—354 yuan vs. our 517—is at first glance surprising, but this category is not as straightforward as it would seem. SSB's figure for regular plus non-regular pay from the work unit is in fact only 10 yuan below ours. In addition to these wage items, however, we include (and SSB evidently does not) several others that appear to have no other representation in the SSB accounts. These include cash income from other jobs, unemployment benefits, income in kind, income received for being a village cadre, and other cash income not from household activities.[11]

Our estimate of income from household production is 15% above the SSB counterpart. This is the average of a 14% difference for farm-type income and a 19% difference for non-farm income. Yet our *gross* income from total household production is only about 5% higher, which suggests that part of the gap between our estimates may be due to different ways of accounting for production costs.

Urban Income

As in 1988, the SSB estimate of urban income is lower than the estimates made from our survey (Table 2.5). The degree of underestima-

TABLE 2.4. Comparison of SSB and Survey Estimates of Rural Income, 1995 (Values in Yuan)

"Per Capita Net Income" of Rural Residents	(1) SSB	(2) Survey	Ratio: (2)/(1)
Total of all items	1,577	2,309	1.46
Labor remuneration	354	517	1.46
Household business			
Farming, animal husbandry, forestry, fishery	937	1,072	1.14
Non-farm activity	188	224	1.19
Private transfer & property	98	99	1.01
Total of items included by SSB	1,577	1,912	1.21
Total of items excluded by SSB		397	

Note: From SSB (1997, p.313) and Table 2.1 above.

TABLE 2.5. Comparison of SSB and Survey Estimates of Urban Income, 1995 (Values in Yuan)

Per Capita Annual Income of Urban Residents	(1) SSB	(2) Survey	Ratio (2)/(1)
Total	4,288	5,706	1.33
Wages	3,324	3,498	1.05
Reemployment of retirees	43	49	1.14
Individual enterprise/sideline	91	30	0.33
Interest, dividends & rent	90	72	0.80
Pensions, subsidies, transfers and special income	740	780	1.05
Total of items included by SSB	4,288	4,429	1.03
Items excluded by SSB (housing subsidy, rental value of owned housing, other net subsidies)		1,277	

Note: From SSB (1997, p. 294) and Table 2.3 above (along with additional information from the survey to reclassify some components of Table 2.3). The SSB has two different concepts of urban income, "per capita income" and "per capita income available for living" (see SSB, 1996, Table 9-5). From the meager explanation of concepts provided by the SSB, it is impossible to know what the difference between them is. In a table of comparative urban and rural per capita incomes, the SSB shows the latter of the two urban measures along with "per capita net income of rural households," suggesting that the two are comparable (SSB, 1996, Table 9-4). After a careful comparison of components, we have decided that "per capita income" is the relevant measure of income which has been used throughout as representing the SSB estimate.

tion is, however, lower in 1995 than in 1988. According to our survey, per capita urban income was 55% higher than the SSB estimate in 1988, and only 33% higher in 1995. The reason for the diminishing difference is the falling proportion of subsidies, which are excluded by the SSB but included by us in urban income.

The understatement by the SSB is largely explained by their exclusion of rental value of owner-occupied housing and subsidies; these components explain 90% of the difference between our estimates and the SSB estimates for 1995. For the items included both by the SSB and by our survey, the aggregate difference between the two estimates is small: the estimate based on the survey is only 3% higher than the SSB estimate. There are, however, significant differences between the two estimates for certain (small) individual components. Our estimate of income from individual and private enterprise is only one-third of the SSB estimate. It should be noted, however, that even the SSB estimates this source of income to be a very small proportion of urban household income.

The real rate of growth of urban income between 1988 and 1995 was only 4.48%, as compared to the SSB estimate of 6.74%! By excluding from the definition of income those components of urban income that declined sharply as a proportion of total income during the period under consideration, the SSB seriously overestimated the nominal rate of growth of urban income. The nominal rate of growth in per capita urban income is 20.1% per year according to the SSB data, compared to 17.5% according to our estimates. Once this is deflated by the annual rate of increase in the urban CPI (12.5%), higher than the rate of increase in rural CPI (11.9%), the rate of growth in urban real income actually falls below the rate of growth in rural real income.

4. Some Implications of the Evidence from the Survey

The findings of the survey reported above have numerous implications for macroeconomic accounting which in turn have important implications for economic policies. This section highlights some of these issues.

Level and Growth of GNP

Available macroeconomic data do not permit a reconciliation of household income estimates with the estimates of GNP and other macroeconomic accounts. It is clear, however, that the official national accounts are substantially understated—a possibility to which analysts have often drawn attention—if our estimates indicate the right order of magnitude of personal income. The weighted average per capita personal income in 1995 was 3,293.9 yuan, or, for a population of 1,211.21 million, 3,989.6 billion yuan. The weighted average household saving rate was 17.25%, yielding an estimated private consumption of 3,301.4 billion yuan, 57.6% of a GNP of 5,727.7 billion yuan estimated by the SSB.[12] The World Bank estimate of the ratio of private consumption to GNP is substantially lower at 46%.[13] If we assume that the World Bank estimate is consistent with the official GNP accounts, substitute our estimate of private consumption for the one implied by the World Bank ratio, and further assume that this is the only source of underestimation of GNP in China, then China's actual GNP should be 11.6% higher than the official estimate. Moreover, the magnitude of different components of GNP would change as shown in Table 2.6.

TABLE 2.6. Macroeconomic Accounts (Percent of GNP)

	"Official Estimates"	Revised Estimates
Private consumption	46	51.6
Government consumption	12	10.8
Savings	42	37.6
Investment	40	35.8
Exports	21	18.8
Imports	19	17.0

Note: "Official estimates" refer to the ones shown in World Bank (1997f) and are virtually identical to the estimates shown in SSB (1997, p. 32). Revised estimates are obtained by dividing the official estimates by the ratio of revised GNP to official GNP (1.116).

According to these revised estimates, China's investment rate is still very high, though lower than in Southeast Asian countries like Thailand (43%) and Malaysia (41%), and closer to the rate in Indonesia (38%), the Republic of Korea (37%), and Hong Kong (35%).[14] Also, the saving rate drops to a more plausible level, though still remaining about as high as in any Asian country.

The rate of growth in the weighted average real per capita household income is higher according to the SSB (5.75% per year) than to us (5.05%). Does this mean that the official national accounts overstate the growth in GDP and GNP? Although we cannot give a confident answer, it appears that no such conclusion is warranted by our findings. The overestimation of the growth rate in household income by the SSB is due to their overstatement of the growth in urban income. This, in turn, is due primarily to their neglect of some declining components—e.g., in-kind housing subsidy and other subsidies—which are transfers and not parts of GDP or GNP.

The Gap Between GNP Growth and Personal Income Growth

According to the official estimates, per capita real GNP in China increased at an annual average rate of 8.07% between 1988 and 1995.[15] The growth in real per capita household income, on the other hand, was only 4.71% for rural China, 4.48% for urban China, and 5.05% for China as a whole.[16] This lag in the growth rate in personal income behind the growth in GNP indicates that the remaining components of GNP (e.g., government and "corporate" incomes) were rising at a much faster rate than GNP. In good part this was due to a rise in the rate of public and "corporate" capital accumulation. Macroeconomic policies in China were redistributing incremental income in favor of accumulation and, generally, government and business.

The difference between the behavior of personal income and that of GNP is a point that is rarely accorded the importance that it deserves. For example, it is widely known that the distribution of income in China has been getting more unequal since the early years of reform.[17] It is, however, quite common to place confidence in the power of the high rate of growth in income to outweigh the adverse effect of the change in the distribution of income in ensuring a continued reduction in the incidence of absolute poverty. Frequently the rate of growth in income that people have in mind in this context is that of GNP, whereas the *relevant* rate is the rate of growth in urban and rural personal income, variables in terms of which poverty thresholds are measured. The change in the distribution of income that can outweigh the effect on the poor of less than 5% growth in average income can be far less dramatic than the change that is required to outweigh the effect of more than 8% growth.

3

The Distribution of Income
· ·
Evolution of Inequality, 1988–1995

1. Introduction

In this chapter we estimate the indices of inequality in the distribution
of per capita household income in rural and urban China, and in China
as a whole, for the year 1995 by using the data from the survey. By
comparing these indices with the ones estimated from the 1988 survey,
we demonstrate the direction and extent of change in the distribution
of income during the intervening period. We also identify the sources
of inequality and their change over the period under review. Finally,
we discuss some of the outstanding aspects of public policy that have
contributed to the evolution of inequality in China.

2. Index of Inequality

As in the 1988 study, the index of inequality used in the present study
is the Gini ratio of per capita household income. The main reasons for
using this index are its easy recognition value; the wide availability of
its estimates both for China's past and for other countries with which
comparisons might be intended, and its relatively few disadvantages as a
useful index of inequality. The value of the Gini ratio conveys an idea of
the degree of inequality independently of the size of the sample on which
the measurement is based, and it avoids the need to make arbitrary welfare judgments. These attributes are not always satisfied by some of the
other measures that are available as alternatives to the Gini ratio.[1]

Apart from the disadvantage that it treats as equivalent changes a
given amount of redistribution at *different* levels of income, the most
serious disadvantage attributed to the Gini ratio is that it can not be

decomposed. There is no simple way of arriving at an estimate of the Gini ratio of the aggregate population from the estimates of the Gini ratios for its constituent groups. Nor is there a way of aggregating the Gini ratios of different sources of income into the Gini ratio of total income. Indirect decomposition of the Gini ratio into contributions made by different sources of income is, however, possible—an attribute of which this study makes extensive use. This is given by the following property of the Gini ratio:

$$G = \Sigma q_i C_i$$

Where G = Gini ratio of total income;

q_i = the ratio of the i-th source of income to total income; and

C_i = the so-called concentration ratio or pseudo-Gini ratio for the i-th source of income.

The concentration ratio for the i-th source of income is estimated exactly the same way from its Lorenz (or rather, "pseudo Lorenz") distribution as the Gini ratio is, except that individuals are ranked in this distribution according to their per capita overall income rather than per capita income from i-th source.[2]

A component of income having a concentration ratio that is greater than the Gini ratio is "disequalizing" in the sense that a rise in its share of total income will increase the Gini ratio, other things remaining equal. The contribution of the i-th source of income to inequality—the percent share of the Gini ratio that is accounted for by the distribution of the i-th source of income—is given by $z_i = 100(q_i C_i)/G$. A component of income that has a z_i greater than its percent share of total income has a disequalizing effect on overall income distribution in the sense that a rise in its share of total income will increase the Gini ratio.

3. Distribution of Rural Income

Table 3.1 shows the Gini ratios and concentration ratios for rural China for both 1988 and 1995. Table 3.2 shows the shares of income and its components accruing to different decile groups of income recipients in rural China for the year 1995.[3]

Rural Inequality and its Sources in 1995

Table 3.1 shows a sharp rise in inequality in rural China between 1988 and 1995.[4] The Gini ratio of income distribution in 1995 is among

TABLE 3.1. Rural Income Inequality and Its Sources

	(1) 100q_i		(2) G or C_i		(3) 100 $(q_iC_i)/G$	
	1988	1995	1988	1995	1988	1995
Wages	8.73	22.38	0.710	0.738	18.3	39.7
Receipts from private & other enterprises	2.40	6.06	0.487	0.543	3.6	7.9
Income from production activities	74.21	56.15	0.282	0.281	61.8	37.9
Farm income	—	(46.44)	—	(0.238)	—	(26.6)
Income from non-farm enterprises	—	(9.71)	—	(0.484)	—	(11.3)
Property income	0.17	0.43	0.484	0.543	0.3	0.6
Rental value of owned housing	9.67	11.61	0.281	0.321	8.0	9.0
Net transfer from state & collectives	−1.90	−0.48	0.052	−1.759	−0.3	2.0
Miscellaneous income	6.71	3.85	0.418	0.337	8.3	3.1
Total income	100.00	100.00	0.338	0.416	100.0	100.0

Note: Column (1), income share of the i-th component in percent; column (2), the index of inequality, the Gini ratio for total income and the concentration ratios for income components; column (3), percent of total inequality contributed by the i-th component of income.

the highest observed Gini ratios in the rural economies of developing Asia.[5]

The most importance source of income inequality in rural China is income from wages. It accounts for 40% of overall inequality in rural income distribution. Wage income is highly concentrated among the high-income groups: the top two deciles of income recipients appropriate 78% of all income from this source. This apparently counterintuitive finding comes about for three reasons: (1) the average wage was high relative to rural per capita income; (2) wage earners were still relatively few; and (3) rural wage employment is probably concentrated in areas where incomes in general are higher.

The next most important disequalizing components of income are receipts from private and other enterprises and property income. These, however, remained a very small proportion of total income, so their contribution to overall inequality was still small. Income from non-farm enterprises owned by households is also disequalizing. The ownership of individual and private non-farm enterprises in rural China is concentrated among the higher income groups.

It is particularly noteworthy that net transfer from the state and the collectives—a negative source of income, signifying that on

TABLE 3.2. Proportions of Income and Its Components Held by Each Decile Group in Rural China in 1995

Decile	RY	RY1	RY2	RY3A	RY3B	RY5	RY6	RY7	RY8
1	0.02335	0.00440	0.00822	0.03284	0.02074	0.02010	0.03924	0.24098	0.02889
2	0.03785	0.00861	0.01857	0.05521	0.03035	0.01214	0.04886	0.24403	0.04278
3	0.04713	0.01106	0.02916	0.06865	0.03928	0.02529	0.05851	0.31491	0.04656
4	0.05618	0.01664	0.04416	0.07897	0.04237	0.03868	0.06879	0.34271	0.06424
5	0.06609	0.02359	0.04604	0.09278	0.05135	0.03217	0.07273	0.39122	0.08400
6	0.07736	0.03577	0.05612	0.10288	0.06491	0.07139	0.08171	0.33947	0.09607
7	0.09188	0.04774	0.07295	0.11678	0.08886	0.10915	0.09364	0.28013	0.10156
8	0.11169	0.07205	0.12854	0.12741	0.11648	0.09022	0.11264	0.17435	0.12140
9	0.14958	0.13380	0.22038	0.13947	0.16785	0.20731	0.15630	−0.00147	0.16041
10	0.33889	0.64633	0.37585	0.18502	0.37783	0.39354	0.26758	−1.32633	0.25409

Note: RY = rural income from all sources; RY1 = individual wages, pensions etc; RY2 = receipts from TVEs & enterprises; RY3A = net income from farming; RY3B = net income from non-farm enterprises; RY4 (self-consumption of food) is a category that was separately identified in 1988 and is included in RY3A in 1995; RY5 = income from property; RY6 = rental value of owned housing; RY7 = net taxes paid to state and collectives; RY8 = other income (private transfer etc.).

average rural households are subject to a positive rate of net "taxation" — exerts the most disequalizing effect on the distribution of income. Its concentration ratio (-1.76) signifies that the burden of net taxes (negative net subsidies) is more than fully borne by the lower income groups. As Table 3.2 shows, the top two deciles are the only income groups that, on the average, receive positive net transfer from the state and the collectives. The extreme regressiveness of the system of transfer is a testimony to the complete lack of focus of public finance on the distribution of income. The pattern is consistent with reports that in poorer localities, particularly those without prosperous township and village enterprises, local governments commonly impose a variety of taxes and fees to support local services.[6]

All other sources of income have an equalizing effect on distribution; that is, the share of these sources of income received by poorer households is greater than their share of total income. Farm production activities are by far the most equalizing source of income; its concentration ratio is the lowest of all components. Household farming, which provides 46.4% of total income, contributes only 26.6% to total inequality of income distribution. Rental value of owned housing and miscellaneous sources of income — largely consisting of private transfers — also have an equalizing effect on the distribution of income.

Figure 3.1 graphically illustrates the extreme cases of equality and inequality in the distribution of rural income components. While the concentration curve for income from family farming closely hugs the "45° line" of perfect income equality, that for wage income bows deeply below it, exhibiting great inequality. The concentration curve for net taxes — a negative income item — soars high above the 45° line, indicating that the poorer households pay a disproportionately high share of taxes; it then falls sharply in representation of the net subsidies received by the richest two deciles of the population.

The rich and the poor in rural China, therefore, have very different compositions of income. The principal sources of income for the rich are wage employment, non-farm entrepreneurship, property income, and transfers from the state and the collectives. For the poor, the main sources of income are farming and rental value of owned housing, and, to a lesser extent, private transfers. Net transfer to the state and collectives is a significant source of income erosion for poor households.

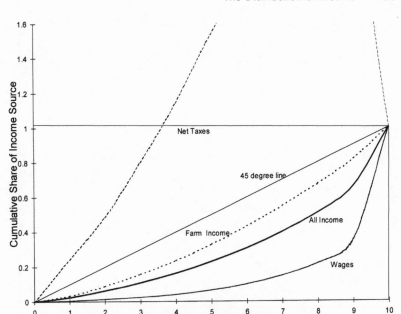

Figure 3.1. Concentration Curves for Wages, Farm Income, and Net Taxes

Change in Income Distribution Between 1988 and 1995

The sharp rise in rural inequality between 1988 and 1995 is illustrated in Figure 3.2, based on the decile distributions in Table 3.2. This increase was due mainly to a change in the *composition* of income—a rise in the share of the disequalizing components of income—rather than a change in inequality of distribution of individual components of income.[7] Had the composition of income in 1995 remained the same as in 1988 while the distribution of each component changed to what it was in 1995, the Gini ratio of rural income distribution would have increased moderately, from 0.338 in 1988 to 0.374 in 1995:

$$\Sigma(1988q_i)(1995C_i) = 0.374$$

On the other hand, had the distribution of each component of income (i.e., its concentration ratio) in 1995 remained the same as in 1988 while the composition of income changed to what it actually was in 1995, the Gini ratio in 1995 would have been nearly as high as it actually was:

$$\Sigma(1995q_i)(1988C_i) = 0.405$$

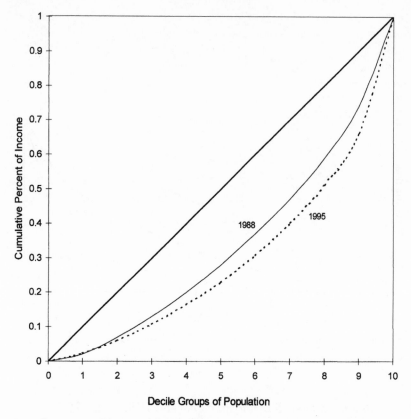

Figure 3.2. Lorenz Curves of Rural Per Capita Income, 1988 and 1995

The single largest source of increased inequality in rural China was the very rapid rise in the share of wages in incremental rural income. The change in the concentration ratio of wages was very small indeed. The same is true of receipts from private and other enterprises and property income, though these remained small as sources of income.

The sharpest increase in the inequality of distribution of a component was in the case of net transfer from state and collectives. In 1988, the distribution of net taxes was merely more "equal" than the distribution of income, signifying a regressive rate of net taxes. In 1995, the regressiveness of net taxes had become massive: the poorest decile's share of net taxes was twelve times its share of income, while the richest decile had a high negative rate of net taxes (net positive transfer from state and collective).

Rental value of owned housing—though still an equalizing source of income in 1995—was significantly less equalizing in 1995 than in 1988. Rural housing assets were becoming concentrated in the hands of richer households. Concentration ratios also increased for wages and, more significant, for property income and receipts from private and other enterprises.

Household production activities, farm and non-farm enterprises together, were as equalizing a source of income in 1995 as in 1988. This implies the continuing egalitarianism of the distribution of income from farming. One of the major explanations of rising inequality in rural China is the slow growth of farming as a source of rural income. The only component of income that became more equalizing in 1995 than in 1988 is income of miscellaneous category. Since this is dominated by private transfers, one is tempted to surmise that income remittances made by migrants mitigated rural inequality to a small extent.

4. Distribution of Urban Income

Table 3.3 shows the Gini ratios for urban income distribution and indices of sources of inequality in urban China in 1988 and 1995.

TABLE 3.3. Urban Income Inequality and Its Sources

	(1) $100q_i$		(2) G or C_i		(3) $100\ (q_iC_i)/G$	
	1988	1995	1988	1995	1988	1995
Cash income of working members	44.42	61.30	0.178	0.247	33.9	45.6
Cash income of retirees	6.83	11.69	0.335	0.316	9.8	11.1
Income from private/ indiv. enterprises	0.74	0.53	0.413	0.042	1.3	0.1
Property income	0.49	1.27	0.437	0.484	0.9	1.9
Housing subsidy	18.14	9.74	0.311	0.516	24.2	15.1
Other net subsidies	20.94	1.25	0.188	0.296	16.9	1.1
Rental value of owned housing	3.90	11.39	0.338	0.639	5.7	21.9
Other (private transfer etc.)	4.53	2.84	0.383	0.371	7.4	3.2
Total income	100.00	100.00	0.233	0.332	100.0	100.0

Note: For an explanation of the columns see notes to Table 3.1. For 1988, other net subsidies include ration coupon subsidies (which ceased to exist in 1995) and other income includes income of non-working members (which also ceased to exist in 1995).

Table 3.4 shows shares of income and its different components held by different decile groups of income recipients in urban China in 1995.[8]

Urban Inequality and Its Sources in 1995

Between 1988 and 1995, the Gini ratio of China's urban income distribution increased sharply. The increase in urban inequality was proportionately greater than the increase in rural inequality over the same period. Our estimate of the urban Gini ratio for 1995 is 18% higher than the official estimate based on the SSB data.[9]

Of the eight sources of urban income identified in Table 3.3, four are disequalizing in the sense that their concentration ratios are higher than the Gini ratio; that is, richer income groups appropriate higher proportions of income from these sources. Of these four, rental value of owned housing and housing subsidy have a quantitatively large effect on overall inequality. Together they account for 37% of the urban Gini ratio, even though they account for only 21% of urban income. The other two disequalizing sources of income—property income and miscellaneous income (private transfers and other sources not specified elsewhere)—together account for 5% of overall inequality while contributing 4% of income.

Wages, the largest source of urban income, still exert an equalizing effect insofar as the concentration ratio remains significantly lower than

TABLE 3.4. Proportions of Income and Its Components Held by Each Decile Group in Urban China, 1995

Decile	UY	UY1	UY2	UY4	UY5	UY6	UY7	UY9	UY10
1	0.03258	0.03877	0.02860	0.16203	0.01364	0.02912	0.03209	0.01287	0.01724
2	0.04879	0.05738	0.04911	0.09298	0.02467	0.04792	0.05882	0.02642	0.02111
3	0.05816	0.06890	0.05257	0.12046	0.04216	0.04736	0.06239	0.03073	0.03070
4	0.06689	0.07781	0.06606	0.03412	0.04885	0.06319	0.06807	0.03987	0.03644
5	0.07596	0.08749	0.07632	0.04953	0.05770	0.06316	0.07131	0.05622	0.03740
6	0.08617	0.09478	0.09852	0.06086	0.07514	0.07723	0.08328	0.07168	0.04453
7	0.09811	0.10832	0.09935	0.06770	0.08818	0.09096	0.10321	0.08446	0.05736
8	0.11482	0.12362	0.12781	0.08136	0.11981	0.11859	0.13167	0.10496	0.06073
9	0.14432	0.13975	0.18855	0.16895	0.15358	0.17658	0.17485	0.16353	0.09356
10	0.27418	0.20318	0.21310	0.16200	0.37628	0.28590	0.21432	0.40927	0.60093

Note: UY = urban income from all sources; UY1 = cash income of working members; UY2 = Cash income of retirees; UY4 = Income from private/individual enterprise; UY5 = Income from property; UY6 = Miscellaneous income; UY7 = Non-housing subsidies including income in kind (net); UY9 = Housing subsidy in kind; UY10 = Rental value of owned housing; UY3 (income of non-working members) and UY8 (ration coupon subsidies) were separate categories in 1988 but ceased to exist in 1995.

the Gini ratio. Except for the top two deciles, all other groups have higher shares of total wage bill than of total income. Cash income of retirees, consisting of pensions and benefits, has a very mildly equalizing effect on overall distribution.

Unexpectedly, and unlike in rural China, income from privately and individually owned enterprises is strongly equalizing. But this appears to be an artifice of the failure of the survey to distinguish between two quite different kinds of private activity that are lumped together in this category: profitable private entrepreneurship providing high incomes to relatively few households, and rudimentary, informal-sector activities providing low incomes to many poor households. Moreover, there are too few observations of the former (private enterprise income alone) to say anything with confidence about its level or distribution. The fact that the combined category has a bimodal distribution in 1995, with high proportions of income appropriated by very low income households and very high income households, but little of it going to middle deciles, does suggest a proliferation of informal sector activities between the two dates. The poorest decile in 1995 receives five times as high a share of this source as of total income. The top two deciles receive as high a share of income from this source as the poorest decile. Clearly, the nature of this source of income differs very substantially between the poor and the rich. The former must be deriving a relatively large proportion of their income from rudimentary, informal activities, while the rich must be deriving their income from more productive private enterprises. It is also clear that informal activities are widespread not only among the floating migrants, who have not been captured by the survey, but also among registered urban residents.

Non-housing subsidies (net of taxes) are mildly equalizing, but their share of total net urban subsidies is very low. Together, all net subsidies have a fairly strongly disequalizing effect on urban income distribution.

Figure 3.3 shows the 1995 Lorenz curve for urban income, together with concentration curves for three categories of urban income, based on the decile distributions in Table 3.4. As in the case of rural income, the equalizing or disequalizing nature of a particular source can be judged by the relation of its concentration curve to the Lorenz curve of all urban income. Thus, wages remain relatively equally distributed, lying inside the Lorenz curve and closer to the 45° line. In contrast, the highly unequal distributions over the urban population of housing subsidy and, especially, rental value of owned housing are portrayed by their deeply bowed curves. As we have seen, well over

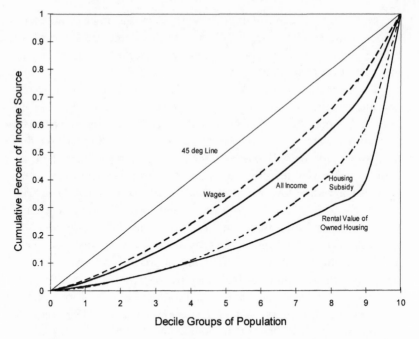

Figure 3.3. Concentration Curves for Components of Urban Income, 1995. See Note to Table 3.1 for definition of "concentration curves." The curve for "Urban Income" is a true Lorenz curve.

half of the latter income source goes to the top decile of the urban population.

Change in Income Distribution between 1988 and 1995

Figure 3.4, presenting the Lorenz curves for urban household per capita income in 1988 and 1995, shows clearly the substantial increase in inequality between those two dates. However, the nature of the increase was somewhat different from that of the rural case.

Unlike the case in rural China, the increase in urban inequality was due entirely to heightened inequality of distribution of individual components of income. The change in the composition of income sources had no role in explaining the rising urban inequality. Had the composition of income in 1995 remained the same as in 1988 and the distribution of individual components changed in the way they did, the inequality of urban income distribution in 1995 would have been exactly equal to its actual value:

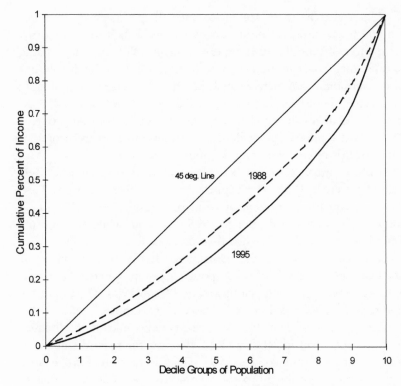

Figure 3.4. Lorenz Curves, Urban Income, 1988 and 1995

$$\Sigma(1988q_i)(1995C_i) = 0.332$$

With the actual composition of income sources in 1995 and the distribution of individual income sources in 1988, there would have been little increase in overall urban inequality between the two periods:

$$\Sigma(1995q_i)(1988C_i) = 0.238$$

Of the eight sources of urban income, the distribution of five became more unequal between 1988 and 1995. There was little change in the distribution of two other components. The distribution of only one component—income from private and individual enterprises—improved sharply, and this result may well be spurious.

Though still an equalizing source of income, wages have become far less equalizing in 1995 than they were in 1988. This was probably a desirable change; previously, the wage spread was kept artificially low to the detriment of work incentives. Greater differentiation in wage structure may well enhance productive efficiency.

Unfortunately, there was no countervailing change in the distribution of net subsidies. Ideally, one would want the income redistributive effect of subsidies to bring down the overall Gini ratio—that is, to cause their concentration ratios to be negative. Had the distribution of net subsidies been merely equal (i.e., had their concentration ratios been zero), the urban Gini ratio in 1995 would have been 0.278 despite all the disequalizing change in the distribution of other sources. This would represent an egalitarian distribution of urban income by the standards of contemporary developing countries.

Instead, urban subsidies became far more disequalizing in 1995 than they were in 1988. This happened for a number of reasons. First, the most equalizing component of urban subsidies in 1988—ration coupons—was abolished prior to 1995.[10] Second, while housing subsidies have been reduced to half their previous level as a proportion of urban household income, their distribution has become sharply more unequal. The top decile of urban population appropriated 41% of all housing subsidies in 1995, compared to 28% in 1988. The concentration ratio of housing subsidies increased by two-thirds.

Rental value of owned housing also became much more disequalizing in 1995 than in 1988. Indeed, this was the most disequalizing component of urban income in 1995. The privatization of urban housing has clearly contributed to a sharp exacerbation of urban inequality. The rich were the major beneficiaries of the program of privatization of the existing stock of public housing. They also had far better access to investment in private housing construction in urban China. The top decile alone had 60% of the rental value of owned housing. In other words, approximately 60% of privately owned housing assets belonged to the richest 10% of the urban population.[11]

Property income doubled its still small contribution to the Gini ratio. It both grew larger as a source of income and became more unequally distributed.[12]

As already noted, income from individual and private enterprise became dramatically more equal in 1995.[13] We have already stated why we do not give much credence to this result. Between 1988 and 1995, the composition of individual and private enterprises in urban China must have undergone a massive change. There has been a proliferation of rudimentary informal activities which provide means of survival to the urban poor.

5. Overall Distribution of Income in China

The overall distribution of income for China was obtained by weighting the rural and urban samples of the 1995 survey so as to represent the relative shares of rural and urban population in 1995.[14] Table 3.5 shows the Gini ratios of income distribution for China as a whole and the concentration ratios of rural and urban income and their components for 1988 and 1995. Table 3.6 shows the proportions of overall income and its components held by each decile group in 1995.[15]

Overall Inequality in China and Its Sources

As in 1988, the Gini ratio for China as a whole is higher than the Gini ratio for either rural or urban China. This means that inequality be-

TABLE 3.5. Overall Income Inequality in China and Its Sources

	(1) 100q_i		(2) G or C_i		(3) 100($q_i C_i$)/G	
	1988	1995	1988	1995	1988	1995
Total Rural Income	(57.10)	(49.09)	0.116	0.192	(17.4)	(20.9)
Wages	4.99	10.71	0.528	0.567	6.9	13.4
Receipts from private & other enterprises	1.37	2.94	0.279	0.301	1.0	2.0
Income from production activities	42.39	27.84	0.053	0.045	5.9	2.8
Farm income	—	(23.04)	—	−0.001	—	(−0.1)
Income from non-farm enterprises	—	(4.80)	—	0.266	—	(2.8)
Property income	0.10	0.22	0.272	0.327	0.1	0.2
Rental value of owned housing	5.52	5.74	0.067	0.090	1.0	1.1
Net transfer from state & collectives	−1.09	−0.26	−0.147	−1.924	0.4	1.1
Miscellaneous income	3.83	1.90	0.214	0.090	2.1	0.4
Total Urban Income	(42.90)	(50.89)	0.735	0.703	(82.5)	(79.1)
Cash income of working members	19.06	31.20	0.715	0.664	35.7	45.8
Cash income of retirees	2.93	5.95	0.773	0.698	5.9	9.2
Income from private/indiv. enterprises	0.32	0.27	0.836	0.516	0.7	0.3
Property income	0.21	0.64	0.810	0.776	0.4	1.1
Housing subsidy	7.78	4.96	0.761	0.789	15.5	8.7
Other net subsidies	8.99	0.63	0.719	0.687	16.9	1.0
Rental value of owned housing	1.67	5.80	0.767	0.840	3.4	10.8
Other (private transfer etc.)	1.94	1.44	0.785	0.719	4.0	2.3
Total Income	100.00	100.00	0.382	0.452	100.0	100.0

Note: See notes to Tables 3.1 and 3.3 for an explanation of columns and other relevant elements.

TABLE 3.6. Proportion of Income and Its Components Held by Each Decile Group in All of China, 1995

Decile	Y	RY	RY1	RY2	RY3A	RY3B	RY5	RY6	RY7	RY8	UY	UY1	UY2
1	0.01874	0.03790	0.00831	0.01461	0.05300	0.03257	0.01969	0.05849	0.30993	0.04762	0.00026	0.00031	0.00004
2	0.03052	0.06121	0.01322	0.03545	0.08931	0.04895	0.02442	0.07644	0.36871	0.06128	0.00092	0.00106	0.00142
3	0.03924	0.07752	0.02364	0.05841	0.10837	0.05996	0.05070	0.09275	0.43355	0.08606	0.00232	0.00266	0.00215
4	0.04882	0.09377	0.03774	0.07178	0.12645	0.07976	0.06009	0.09864	0.45199	0.12025	0.00546	0.00609	0.00492
5	0.06048	0.10974	0.05447	0.07866	0.14100	0.09990	0.10083	0.11663	0.33443	0.12576	0.01297	0.01611	0.00866
6	0.07565	0.11981	0.07968	0.12458	0.13914	0.11857	0.12893	0.11878	0.24486	0.12634	0.03305	0.03939	0.03322
7	0.09596	0.10555	0.08423	0.16697	0.10366	0.10704	0.10946	0.10887	0.03847	0.13039	0.08670	0.10167	0.08374
8	0.12497	0.09373	0.10019	0.12943	0.07987	0.10651	0.15641	0.09824	-0.08603	0.09301	0.15509	0.17781	0.15872
9	0.16867	0.10082	0.15244	0.12280	0.06758	0.11834	0.12630	0.10330	-0.19798	0.08390	0.23411	0.25722	0.25343
10	0.33696	0.19994	0.44607	0.19730	0.09163	0.22839	0.22317	0.12786	-0.89793	0.12540	0.46912	0.39766	0.45369

Decile	UY4	UY5	UY6	UY7	UY9	UY10
1	0.00000	0.00000	0.00099	0.00075	0.00022	0.00005
2	0.00459	0.00014	0.00069	0.00059	0.00002	0.00037
3	0.02275	0.00049	0.00337	0.00172	0.00081	0.00099
4	0.06240	0.00176	0.00496	0.00599	0.00246	0.00305
5	0.03547	0.00726	0.01141	0.01322	0.00498	0.00728
6	0.08869	0.01498	0.02930	0.03687	0.01318	0.01566
7	0.16157	0.05707	0.07649	0.09559	0.04939	0.04246
8	0.09558	0.11518	0.14083	0.14949	0.10867	0.08016
9	0.17096	0.21202	0.21835	0.23872	0.19602	0.13134
10	0.35799	0.59110	0.51361	0.45708	0.62425	0.71865

Note: Y is income for all China. For an explanation of RY, UY, and their components, see tables 3.2 and 3.4.

tween urban and rural China continues to dominate inequality within each of them. The dominance of urban/rural inequality was, however, weaker in 1995 than in 1988; the overall Gini ratio for China in 1995 was 21% higher than the average of rural and urban Gini ratios in 1995, whereas it was 34% higher in 1988. Similarly, the gap between the overall Gini ratio, on the one hand, and each of rural and urban Gini ratios, on the other, was much lower in 1995 than in 1988.

By the evidence of the Gini ratio, China was among the more unequal societies in developing Asia by the middle of the 1990s. The Gini ratio for China in 1995 — 0.452 — is higher than the Gini ratios for India, Pakistan, and Indonesia, and perhaps about the same as the Gini ratio for the Philippines.[16] Our estimate of the Gini ratio for China is 9% higher than the estimate reported by the World Bank for the same year (0.415).[17]

The concentration ratios for rural income and most of its components are low, indicating that a redistribution in favor of the rural economy, other things remaining equal, would reduce inequality for China as a whole. The only component of rural income that is disequalizing for China as a whole is wages. Even those other components of rural income that have a disequalizing effect on *rural* income distribution — for example, income from non-farm enterprises, property income, or receipts from private and other enterprises — have an equalizing effect on overall income distribution for China. A rise in their share of total income would make rural income distribution more unequal but, at the same time, would reduce inequality of income distribution for China as a whole.

Change in Income Distribution Between 1988 and 1995

Although there was little change in the ratio of rural per capita income to urban per capita income, the share of rural household income in China's aggregate household income fell from 57.1% in 1988 to 49.1% in 1995. This was due to increased urbanization. The fall in rural households' share in China's aggregate household income contributed to an increase in the Gini ratio for China as a whole. Had rural households' share of China's household income in 1995 remained the same as in 1988, the Gini ratio for China in 1995 would have been 0.411 — or 9% lower than the actual ratio — given the actual intrarural and intraurban changes in inequality.

Rural income remains strongly equalizing for China's income distribution, but it is less equalizing in 1995 than it was in 1988. This is because several components of rural income have become more disequalizing (less equalizing) over time. Wages are quantitatively the most important of these components. Others are net taxes (negative net transfers), receipts from private and other enterprises, property income, and rental value of owned housing.

Urban income continues to be highly disequalizing for China as a whole, but it is less so in 1995 than it was in 1988. This is true of all components of urban income except two; rental value of owned housing and housing subsidy. The disequalizing effect of these two components on China's overall inequality has increased between 1988 and 1995.

6. Regional Inequality

Urban/Rural Inequality

Official estimates by the SSB show a sharp rise in urban/rural disparity in per capita income between 1988 and 1995 (Table 3.7). The extent of this inequality in China has been greater than in most Asian developing countries, and the results of our 1988 survey showed that the SSB understated the extent of urban/rural disparity.[18] The results of the 1995 survey, however, show the opposite: the official estimates over-

TABLE 3.7. Growth of Urban and Rural Income

	Survey Estimates	SSB Estimates
Growth in nominal income (percent per year)		
Rural	17.20	16.40
Urban	17.52	20.07
Growth in real income (percent per year)		
Rural	4.71	4.00
Urban	4.48	6.74
Growth in CPI (percent per year)		
Rural	11.93	11.93
Urban	12.49	12.49
Urban per capita income as multiple of rural per capita income		
1988: Nominal	2.42	2.19
1995: Nominal	2.47	2.72
At 1988 cost of living	2.38	2.63

Note: Data for the survey estimates are from Tables 2.1 and 2.3 and sources indicated therein. Data for SSB estimates are from SSB (1989, 1996). Growth in CPI is based on the data in Table 2.2.

state the extent of the urban/rural income gap. As shown above, the SSB as seriously overstates the rate of growth in urban income as it understates the rate of growth of rural income. Thus, the SSB estimates show a rise in urban/rural income ratio, from 2.19 in 1988 to 2.72 in 1995 in nominal terms. In contrast, the estimates from our survey yield a rate of growth in nominal urban income that is only slightly higher than the rate of growth in nominal rural income. In nominal terms, the ratio of urban per capita income to rural per capita income increases modestly, from 2.42 in 1988 to 2.47 in 1995.

The estimated changes in income disparity at constant purchasing power are, however, different because of the difference in the increase between rural and urban consumer price indices (CPIs). Between 1988 and 1995, the rate of increase in urban CPI per year was about half a percentage point higher than the rate of increase in rural CPI. According to the SSB data, the urban/rural income disparity at constant 1988 purchasing power increased from 2.19 to 2.63. According to our survey results, at constant 1988 purchasing power, the ratio of per capita urban income to per capita rural income declined modestly from 2.42 in 1988 to 2.38 in 1995.

The exclusion of the floating migrants appears to contribute to an overstatement of the urban/rural income gap. It is, however, not at all clear how it affects the estimated *change* in urban/rural income gap between 1988 and 1995.

The above conclusion should be qualified. According to the SSB estimates, 1995 witnessed the first reversal of a trend rise in the ratio of urban income to rural income, which peaked in 1994 at 2.87. Notwithstanding the bias in the SSB definition, this probably indicates that the ratio between incomes according to our definition was also higher in 1994 than in 1995. This is also strongly suggested by the improvement in agriculture's terms of trade in 1995 and by the achievement of a rate of growth in agricultural production in 1995 which was the highest in a decade.[19]

To conclude, urban/rural inequality in China was already extremely high in 1988.[20] Since 1988, there probably was a further modest rise in inequality to 1994. By 1995, the urban/rural inequality in per capita income, at constant purchasing power, had become slightly lower than in 1988, though still remaining extremely high by international standards.

Interprovincial Inequality

Although the period between 1988 and 1995 was not characterized by a rise in inequality between average urban and average rural incomes, there was a sharp rise in another kind of regional inequality: the inequality between rich and poor provinces. Data from our survey cannot adequately document this because we do not cover all the provinces. Moreover, as noted in Chapter 1, the sizes of our provincial samples are not always large enough to derive provincial measurements with an acceptably low sampling error. Therefore, the confidence that we can place on the provincial estimates is lower than the confidence that we can place on overall rural and urban estimates.

It is, however, not surprising that the rates of growth of provincial household incomes from our survey differ from those estimated by the official survey. It is also possible that the excluded components are "income elastic"; that is, they have grown faster (or fallen at a slower rate) in the rapidly growing provinces. This explains the sharper increase in interprovincial inequality according to our survey estimates than according to the official estimates.

We do not have an overt concern about the difference between our relative levels of provincial incomes, but there is at least one extreme result—the high negative growth in per capita income in Hunan—that would inevitably raise eyebrows. Have we seriously understated Hunan's income? It is, of course, possible for this to have happened if, for example, the sample counties in Hunan were far poorer than the average. While conceding this possibility, we would like to note a few other relevant facts. Hunan's per capita rural income was 93% of the average for rural China, according to the SSB. It is only 66.4% according to our estimate. As noted in Chapter 2, the three main components of ours that are either excluded or seriously undercovered by the SSB are rental value of owned housing, net taxes, and "wages." If these three components are excluded, Hunan's per capita rural income according to our estimate becomes as high as 87% of the average for rural China. The low income for Hunan is largely explained by its exceptionally low income from rental value of housing (39.7% of the average for rural China), wages (28.6% of rural China) and net taxes, a negative source of income (463.3% of that for rural China). Although we still cannot rule out the possibility that the low income estimate for rural Hunan is substantially due to a biased provincial sample, the above findings warrant the suspicion that the official estimate may have seriously overstated the relative level and the growth rate of income for that province.

Table 3.8 shows the ratios of per capita incomes between the richest and the poorest provinces *included in our 1995 survey*, accord-

TABLE 3.8. Distribution of Per Capita Provincial Incomes: Ranges and Coefficients of Variation

	Ratios of Per Capita Income between the Richest and Poorest Provinces				Coefficient of Variation of Provincial Per Capita Income			
	Our Survey		SSB		Our Survey		SSB	
	1988	1995	1988	1995	1988	1995	1988	1995
Rural	2.69	4.60	2.42	3.66	0.33	0.55	0.35	0.41
Urban	2.19	2.93	—	2.25	0.37	0.46	—	0.30

Note: The source of data for SSB estimates are SSB (1989, 1996). For 1988, estimates of provincial urban incomes are not available from SSB sources. The poorest rural province is Gansu and the richest is Beijing. The poorest urban province is Shanxi and the richest Guangdong. These rankings are for the provinces included in the 1995 survey. For urban China these ranks were the same in 1988. For rural China the relative ranks of Gansu and Beijing were the same in 1988, although the survey of that year covered additional provinces, including Heilongjiang (poorer than Gansu) and Zhejiang, Tianjin, and Shanghai (all richer than Beijing).

ing to the SSB and according to our survey. Both the SSB data and the results of our survey show a sharp increase in the range of provincial incomes for rural China. The SSB estimate of the rise (51%) is, however, far lower than the rise estimated by our survey (71%). For urban China, there is no SSB range estimate for 1988; SSB's estimate for 1995 is only three-quarters as high as ours. It is impossible to determine to what extent the differences in the estimates of range represent a downward bias in the estimated regional inequality according to the SSB as a result of its incomplete definition of income, and to what extent they stem from larger sampling errors in our estimates.

The rural coefficient of variation of our survey is roughly the same as that of the SSB in 1988, but it too increases much faster than SSB's. Our estimates of the coefficient of variation for both rural and urban incomes in 1995 are substantially higher than the official ones. Even according to the latter, however, it is clear that, while part of the sharp increase in absolute interregional inequality in incomes has been matched by increases in average income, *relative* regional inequality has nevertheless also grown substantially.[21]

Intraprovincial Inequality

It is useful to begin the reporting of the provincial Gini ratios (Table 3.9) by repeating that the relatively small size of the provincial samples leads us to place less confidence in these estimates than in the national

TABLE 3.9. Regional Inequality

	Per Capita Income 1995 (Yuan)	Real Income Growth 1988–1995, % per year	Gini Ratio	
			1988	1995
Rural				
Gansu	1138	1.25	0.263	0.359
Guizhou	1213	0.72	0.295	0.304
Shanxi	1408	0.85	0.320	0.324
Shaanxi	1477	3.65	0.289	0.398
Yunnan	1516	1.26	0.287	0.299
Hunan	1533	-3.30	0.255	0.302
Sichuan	1583	0.62	0.265	0.340
Jiangxi	1801	1.68	0.230	0.287
Anhui	1827	3.79	0.249	0.272
Henan	1872	6.45	0.299	0.275
Hubei	1922	1.98	0.231	0.311
Hebei*	2057	2.54	0.293	0.282
Liaoning*	2172	2.02	0.330	0.337
Jilin	2376	7.26	0.354	0.338
Shandong*	2745	7.89	0.285	0.432
Zhejiang*	4270	4.86	0.286	0.362
Jiangsu*	4507	11.66	0.383	0.375
Guangdong*	4522	7.11	0.306	0.390
Beijing*	5240	9.33	0.305	0.305
Urban				
Shanxi	3737	2.51	0.207	0.256
Henan	3927	2.37	0.194	0.284
Anhui	4436	3.41	0.194	0.223
Yunnan	4717	2.81	0.188	0.223
Hubei	4846	3.34	0.163	0.233
Sichuan	4936	—	—	0.264
Liaoning*	5630	4.94	0.145	0.299
Gansu	5665	3.94	0.215	0.482
Jiangsu*	5982	5.53	0.162	0.236
Beijing*	9276	7.84	0.186	0.264
Guangdong*	10938	6.86	0.249	0.316

Note: Asterisks denote coastal provinces and Beijing which were major beneficiaries of globalization. Real growth has been estimated by deflating 1995 income by the rise in cost of living between 1988 and 1995 (120.09% for rural China and 127.90% for urban China, according to official CPI) and estimating the compounded annual rate of growth between 1988 and 1995. Per capita incomes for 1988 are shown in Khan et al., 1993.

estimates. There is a great deal of variability among the provincial Gini ratios. The variability is greater for 1995 than for 1988, as shown by the following coefficients of variation:

	Rural	Urban
1988	0.127	0.158
1995	0.139	0.275

It is, however, not possible to find any pattern to the variation in provincial Gini ratios. They do not vary systematically with the level of per capita income. The average Gini ratio for the "coastal provinces" for 1995 is insignificantly different from the average for all the provinces.[22] Nor can we find any particular pattern regarding the composition of income sources.

Of the nineteen provinces in the rural survey, fifteen experienced an increase in the Gini ratio between 1988 and 1995. In nine of these fifteen cases, the increase was more than 10%. In four cases, the Gini ratio declined. In only one case did the reduction in the Gini ratio exceed 5%. Again, there is no obvious way to relate the differences among the provinces in the rate of change in inequality to any of their other characteristics. The Gini ratio increased in all ten provinces in the urban survey for which information is available about the change between 1988 and 1995. With the exception of Anhui and Yunnan, the rise in the Gini ratio exceeded 20% everywhere.

7. Summary of Findings

The surveys of 1988 and 1995 serve as a far better empirical foundation for the analysis of the nature, extent, evolution, and sources of inequality in China than does anything else that is available to date. The incompleteness of the definition of income and the absence of details in data from official surveys are definite obstacles to an adequate understanding of the level of inequality in China and changes in it.

During the period between 1988 and 1995, inequality in the distribution of income in China increased sharply. By 1995, China had become one of the more unequal of the Asian developing countries. Inequality in income distribution is now greater in China than in countries like India, Pakistan, and Indonesia, and probably as high as in the Philippines.

Inequality has increased both in rural and urban China. The rate of increase in inequality has been higher in urban than in rural areas, although the degree of inequality still remains lower in the former. The increase in urban inequality appears to have been more uniform among the provinces than has the increase in rural inequality.

In rural China, wage employment is the most important source of inequality. Other disequalizing sources of income, in decreasing order of importance, are income from non-farm entrepreneurship, receipts from private and other enterprises, and property income. Farm income and rental value of owned housing are the major equalizing sources of rural income. Rural households are subject to a highly regressive rate of net "taxation" (negative net transfer from the state and collectives), which has an adverse effect on the distribution of income.

The increase in rural inequality between 1988 and 1995 has been due mainly to a change in the composition of rural income in favor of the disequalizing components, especially wages, and to a far lesser extent to increasing inequality in the distribution of individual components of income. The distribution of a majority of components has, however, become worse over the period under review.

The most important sources of urban inequality are rental value of owned housing and housing subsidy. The highly disequalizing distribution of net "subsidies" (net transfer by the state and collectives in cash and kind) indicates a complete lack of focus of public finance on the distribution of income. Income from individual and private enterprise has unexpectedly turned into the most equalizing source of income in urban China, signifying both our failure to capture adequately pure private entrepreneurial income and a widespread prevalence of rudimentary informal activities that have been captured under this heading.

Unlike the case of rural China, the increase in urban inequality between 1988 and 1995 has been due to greater inequality in the distribution of individual sources of income. Changes in the composition of income had no role in this process. Differentiation in the structure of wages was the single most important source of increasing urban inequality. This in itself was desirable insofar as the enforced egalitarianism of the structure of labor remuneration in the past was inconsistent with incentive and efficiency. What is hard to justify is that, instead of implementing compensatory measures to limit inequality, public policy actually aggravated inequality by instituting a highly disequalizing system of net subsidies and by promoting a housing reform that created an extremely unequal distribution of housing assets. Most of the components of urban income became more disequalizing (less equalizing) over the period under review. The one exception was income from individual and private enterprise, a phenomenon that has been commented on above.

Overall inequality in China is greater than either rural or urban inequality, indicating the dominance of urban/rural disparity over intrarural and intraurban inequality. The dominance of urban/rural disparity was, however, a little lower in 1995 than in 1988. A redistribution of income in favor of the rural society would reduce overall inequality in China as long as this was not brought about exclusively or mainly by an expansion of wage employment. With the exception of wages, all sources of rural income have an equalizing effect on China's overall income distribution. All sources of urban income have a disequalizing effect on the overall income distribution, and this effect is strongest for rental value of owned housing and housing subsidy.

The increase in overall inequality between 1988 and 1995 is largely explained by the increasing importance of rural wage employment and the increasing inequality of distribution of all the components of urban income. Net transfers from (or to) the state and the collectives to (or from) both urban and rural households have exacerbated overall inequality in China.

There have been two important spatial sources of inequality in China: the inequality between urban and rural sectors, and the inequality among provinces. During the period under review, the contribution of urban/rural disparity to overall inequality does not appear to have changed significantly. There was, however, an aggravation of interprovincial inequality which was an important source of exacerbation of inequality.

Our estimate of the *change* in the overall Gini ratio is broadly in agreement with similar estimates made by others (e.g., the World Bank), although the *levels* of the Gini ratio estimated by these others are somewhat lower. In our view, their lower levels result from the fact that they are based on the official survey data, which suffer from an inappropriate definition of income and the availability of data only for highly aggregated groups and not for individual households. These other sources cannot "decompose" inequality into its sources because the official survey data do not show the distribution of components of income. We are, therefore, unable to compare our results about the sources of inequality with any alternative set of estimates.

4

Trends in the Incidence of Poverty
· ·

1. Introduction

Available Evidence on Poverty Trends

In Chapter 1, we argued that there was a major shift in China's development policy around the middle of the 1980s. Before that time, China's reform program was focused on the rural economy, and the growth of the latter was the principal element of China's economic growth. Since the middle of the 1980s, China's development strategy has increasingly been focused on a closer integration with the rapidly globalizing world economy, and China's growth has been concentrated in non-agricultural activities. The distributional consequences of growth on China's poor have been very different in the two periods. During the initial period of reform, until about 1985, China achieved a rapid reduction in the incidence of poverty. After the mid-1980s, the rate of reduction in poverty drastically slowed and arguably was halted or even reversed. There is a broad agreement among all analysts about a break in the trend in poverty reduction in the mid-1980s, although there is some disagreement, especially between the official sources and the rest, about the nature and extent of the slowdown in the rate of poverty reduction after that date.

A detailed World Bank study estimated that the proportion of rural population in poverty declined from 33% of rural population in 1978 to 11% in 1984. Thereafter, there was no trend change in the ratio, which remained as high as 11.5% in 1990, the terminal year of the study. The World Bank's estimate of the urban population in poverty similarly shows a decline from 1.9% in 1981 to 0.3% in 1984 and no trend decline thereafter, the ratio being 0.3% in 1990.[1]

One of the present writers made estimates of poverty for rural and urban China for the period 1980–1994 by using the SSB's grouped data on personal income distribution.[2] Table 4.1 shows three different indices of poverty that have been estimated for rural and urban China. The first is the Head-Count (HC) index, showing the number of persons belonging to households with per capita incomes below the poverty threshold as a proportion of the total population of all households. The second is the Proportionate Poverty Gap (PPG) index, which is the average proportionate shortfall in income from the poverty threshold for the entire population, the shortfall for the non-poor being defined as zero. The third measure, the Weighted Poverty Gap (WPG) index, is estimated by first summing, for all the poor, the *squared* gap between the poverty threshold and income as a proportion of the poverty threshold, and then dividing the sum by total population.

Each of these indices provides useful information about the poor. The HC index, the most widely used measure of poverty, simply quantifies the proportion of population in poverty in the sense of having too little income to satisfy basic nutritional and other consumption needs. It is possible for the number of poor to remain unchanged while the average shortfall of their income from the poverty threshold changes; in this case, the HC index would be misleading as an indicator of the change in the condition of the poor. The latter is captured by the PPG index, which is in fact the product of the HC index and the average proportionate income gap of those who are in poverty. It is

TABLE 4.1. Khan's 1996 Poverty Estimates for China

Year	Rural Poverty Indices			Urban Poverty Indices		
	HC	PPG	WPG	HC	PPG	WPG
1980	40.80	11.16	4.25	—	—	—
1981	30.34	7.30	2.64	20.08	3.30	0.94
1983	14.32	2.89	0.82	—	—	—
1985	14.04	3.13	0.98	12.70	2.61	0.98
1988	16.09	4.07	1.45	—	—	
1989	—	—	—	7.42	1.67	0.77
1990	13.87	2.77	0.75	7.39	1.25	0.30
1991	—	—	—	4.73	1.04	0.48
1992	13.63	2.85	0.81	—	—	—
1993	14.11	3.61	1.47	—	—	—
1994	13.62	3.47	1.42	5.90	0.85	0.17

Note: HC = Head Count index; PPG = Proportionate Poverty Gap index; WPG = Weighted Poverty Gap index. From Khan (1996). Of the two different sets of poverty thresholds for which estimates are made, the ones reported here refer to the lower thresholds (i.e., the more extreme poverty).

possible for the number of poor and the average income of the poor to remain unchanged while the distribution of income among the poor improves (the extreme poor gain at the cost of the moderately poor) or deteriorates (the moderately poor gain at the cost of the extreme poor). Policymakers need to monitor this kind of change, which is not captured by the HC index or the PPG index. The WPG index, which rises when the distribution of income among the poor worsens and falls when the distribution improves, reflects such changes accurately. By itself, however, this index has a drawback in that it lacks the intuitively transparent interpretation possessed by the other two indices.[3]

According to these estimates, China's very high rate of growth in the early years of reform was accompanied by a remarkably rapid reduction in the incidence of poverty. In rural China, the pace of reduction in poverty drastically slowed in the mid-1980s and came to a halt in the early 1990s. In urban China, poverty continued to diminish until the end of the 1980s; since then, however, the reduction in urban China also drastically slowed. Given the very large majority of Chinese who live in rural areas, it is right to conclude that, for the country as a whole, the rate of poverty reduction diminished sharply in the mid-1980s and came to a halt in the early 1990s. This is an extraordinary outcome, in view of the fact that the rate of growth in China's per capita GDP continued to accelerate throughout the period to reach a height that is almost unprecedented in human history.[4]

How do these results accord with other estimates of poverty trends in China? Official estimates of rural poverty are made by the SSB, which does not publicize the details of its methodology.[5] For 1985, the SSB estimates the number of rural poor to be 125 million, which is higher than the estimates presented in the studies discussed above. The SSB estimates confirm that the rate of decline in rural poverty slowed down appreciably after 1985; however, they claim that the reduction in poverty continued to take place in rural China after 1987, albeit at a much slower rate than before.[6] In the absence of information about the SSB methodology, it is impossible to explain the difference between their estimate of the trend and the estimates made by others. While certain other estimates by Chinese scholars arrive at similar results as the SSB's by making an inadequate adjustment in poverty threshold for rising cost of living, the SSB's cost of living adjustment does not seem to suffer from the same problem.[7]

For urban poverty, the *trends* shown in Table 4.1 are similar to those reported by others, but the *levels* stand out as being much higher than those reported by SSB and the World Bank, especially in the earlier years. Thus, the World Bank estimated that the urban head count rate of poverty was 1.5% in 1981 and declined to 0.1% in 1986 before stagnating at 0.2–0.3% for the rest of the decade (World Bank, 1992b, p. 140).[8] The figures for 1981 and 1985 are also in conflict with common impressions, based on our institutional knowledge of urban China. Before the reform period began, the size of the urban population was strictly controlled by a system of household registration and the rationing of food. Virtually the entire urban population was employed in the public sector and covered by an extensive system of subsidies. The institutionalized separation of urban and rural populations and the privileges accorded to the former are discussed extensively elsewhere in this book, and they are the basis for our finding of a very high urban-rural income gap. They seem quite inconsistent with a finding that one-fifth of the urban population in 1981 and 13% of it in 1985 lived in absolute poverty.

That the urban poverty rates for 1981 and 1985 given above are most likely too high is due in part to a poverty threshold which is very high relative to urban per capita income (72% and 53%, respectively, in 1981 and 1985), and which does not take into account the subsidies that, while not included in official income estimates, nevertheless constituted a significant fraction of urban residents' real income in the 1980s. Someone with measured income equal to the poverty threshold in fact had a significantly higher real income when those subsidies are included. Later on, in the 1990s, when urban subsidies had been greatly diminished, the degree of downward distortion in the official income figures lessened. On the other hand, the poverty line used by the World Bank—at only 23% of average urban per capita income in 1985—is so low as to define urban poverty out of existence. We return to this point in our discussion of poverty thresholds below.

There is general agreement that China's growth in the period since the mid-1980s has been far less poverty-alleviating than before, but there is a diversity of views about the reasons for the change. The official Chinese view seems to suggest that remaining poverty in China is localized in remote and resource-poor rural areas, a view that appears consistent with the World Bank's assessment.[9] Yet there is increasing media recognition of what appears to be a growing problem of urban poverty in the 1990s, associated especially with growing layoffs of state enterprise workers. Khan (1996), moreover, argues that the shift of

China's development strategy toward greater integration with the world economy has led to a more disequalizing pattern of growth during the transition period. These are important issues which deserve detailed analysis, but only after we have addressed the issue of whether there are serious questions about the existing estimates of poverty in China.

Limitations of the Existing Poverty Estimates

All the available estimates of poverty in China are based on the data reported in a summary form from the SSB surveys of household income. There are very important deficiencies in these data. As we noted in the previous section and discussed in detail in Chapter 2, they exclude from household income numerous elements that standard accounting elsewhere normally includes. This is a particularly serious problem because the excluded components, as a proportion of household income, have been changing rapidly with the progress of reform in China. This can seriously bias estimates of distribution of income and poverty.

Another problem is that these SSB data are reported for highly aggregated income groups, with the format of reporting varying from one year to another. The number of income classes for which the data are reported has been very limited for earlier years, leading to serious problems of comparability of groups at higher real levels of income. This inevitably compounds errors in estimation.

The quality and quantity of distributional data are not the only problems facing the estimation of poverty trends in China. Another serious problem relates to the lack of transparency of the estimates of consumer price indices (CPI). This makes it very difficult to estimate poverty thresholds over time as indices of a *constant level* of real income.

It is because the above questions plague existing poverty estimates that we now revisit the subject, using new evidence that permits us to avoid many of these problems.

New Evidence

Our surveys for 1988 and 1995 provide a unique set of data to analyze poverty trends in China during the intervening period. They permit estimates of income that are free of many of the deficiencies found in the official data. They cover a period of one of the most breathtakingly rapid rates of growth and integration with the global economy in modern times. The surveys also provide a good deal of information to help identify the characteristics of the poor and the correlates of poverty trends.

2. Estimating Poverty Thresholds

Not all problems of estimating the indices of poverty are resolved by the availability of better data on income and its distribution. The surveys of 1988 and 1995 do not provide necessary information either to estimate poverty thresholds—for example, by fitting Engel functions between levels of nutrition and income—or to endogenously derive CPIs for households at the poverty threshold. These tasks must still be done by using the data from existing official sources.

Estimating Poverty Thresholds for 1995

We use 1995 as the base year for the estimation of the poverty thresholds and then obtain the poverty thresholds for 1988 by using the CPI to deflate them. This method is adopted because more information is available for 1995 than for 1988 concerning the aspects that need to be taken into account in determining the poverty thresholds.

A poverty threshold represents a cut-off standard, in terms of income, consumption, or other characteristics, below which a person is considered poor. In the final analysis, such standards must reflect the judgment and preference of the individual or the agency setting them. Although these judgements and preferences might be based on careful consideration and sensible criteria, there is no escape from the fact that the procedure is essentially arbitrary, for a number of reasons. First, it is difficult or impossible to specify a physiological minimum consumption level necessary to sustain life.[10] Second, absolute poverty lines, though so designated in order to distinguish them from poverty lines based on the income of the lowest x percent of the population, are always in fact relative, in the sense that they express a society's judgment at a particular point in time as to what constitutes a minimum acceptable living standard. That judgment differs among countries and can change over time within a country. We return to this point later in discussing the difference in living standards embodied in our rural and urban poverty thresholds.

Because of the essential arbitrariness of particular poverty thresholds, researchers and planners who must make poverty estimates tend to focus more on the *change* in the incidence of poverty over time than on its *level* at any particular time. Moreover, they often use multiple thresholds which reflect alternative standards of demarcating the poor from the non-poor. This is the route that we take, as well.

The most common practice in estimating poverty thresholds is to relate them to the level of income/expenditure that is necessary to satisfy a minimum level of consumption. Two widely used procedures are (1) to estimate, from Engel functions fitted to cross-section data, the level of income/expenditure that would enable a typical person to achieve a specified minimum level of nutrition; and (2) to estimate the cost of a basket of food and non-food goods, within the constraints imposed by consumer preference, that represents a minimum living standard to enable a person to escape poverty. For China, the first method cannot be applied for want of necessary statistical information. The SSB data on rural household expenditure do not provide information on the pattern of consumption for different income groups that is necessary to estimate the Engel function. For urban China, some amount of information is available about the consumption pattern of eight different fractile groups. There are, however, serious problems of using fitted Engel functions based on these data. The income elasticity of food energy consumption estimated from these data is very low, so that a small difference in the threshold defined in terms of nutrition leads to a very large difference in the corresponding income poverty threshold. Furthermore, the estimated elasticity varies rather sharply from one year to another.[11]

Our method of determining the poverty thresholds is a variant of the second of the two procedures listed above. It involves the following steps: (1) a normative minimum of food energy requirement in kilocalories per day for an average person is set; (2) this is multiplied by the estimated actual cost of food energy consumed by the income group that seems to be closest to the poverty threshold, thereby making an allowance for consumer preference; and (3) a further allowance is made for non-food consumption expenditure on the basis of the consumption pattern of the group that seems to be closest to the poverty threshold.

The actual implementation of this method involved numerous difficulties which had to be resolved by making judgments whose accuracy is far from assured. For rural China, we use alternative sets of assumptions about the above parameters, as set out in Table 4.2, to derive a set of alternative thresholds.[12] Note that these alternative assumptions give rise to two thresholds, which we dub the "high" and "low" poverty thresholds, respectively. The low threshold is equal to 70% of the high one. To fill out our menu of choices, we also specify an "inter-

TABLE 4.2. Derivation of Rural Poverty Thresholds

	Low Threshold	High Threshold
Food energy standard (kcal per day)	2,100	2,150
Unit annual cost of 1 kcal (RMB)	0.258	0.323
Ratio of expenditure on food to disposable income	0.67	0.60
Poverty threshold (RMB)	810	1,159

mediate" threshold between the two, equal to 80% of the high threshold; the intermediate threshold comes to 926 yuan.

For urban China, the per capita daily food energy requirement is set at 2,100 kilocalories for all poverty thresholds, not just the high one. The justification for a lower food energy requirement per capita in urban than in rural China is the lower labor force participation per capita and the possible lower intensity of work in urban China as compared to rural China.

For urban China, the SSB provides food consumption data for decile and quintile groups. With less uncertainty than in the rural case regarding the appropriate parameters for the poor, we need to build only one initial poverty threshold. We assume that the households representing the poorest decile of urban population have the same food consumption pattern as the households at the urban poverty threshold. The unit cost of a kilocalorie for this group is estimated to be 0.60 yuan, and food is estimated to account for 55% of consumption for this group. These parameters provide an estimated urban high poverty threshold of 2,291 yuan. We then identify intermediate and low urban thresholds as the values equal to 80% and 70% of this value, respectively.[13]

There are a number of issues that need to be addressed. Our estimates generate ratios of urban to rural poverty thresholds that range from 1.4 up to 2.8 (Table 4.3). Although we cannot make a reasonable estimate of the level of urban income that represents a living standard comparable to a given level of rural income, it is obvious that the difference between the two is closer to the bottom of this range (1.4) than to the top (2.8). The urban (rural) consumption bundle at poverty threshold is unlikely to cost nearly twice as much at urban prices as at rural prices, let alone almost three times as much. What, then, is the justification for such large differences between the higher urban poverty threshold and the higher rural threshold?

TABLE 4.3. Poverty Thresholds and Per Capita Incomes, 1995 (Values in Yuan)

	Per Capita Income	Poverty Threshold	Ratio of Poverty Threshold to Per Capita Income
Rural	2308.63	810 (RLPT)	0.35
		1157 (RHPT)	0.50
Urban	5706.19	1604 (ULPT)	0.28
		2291 (UHPT)	0.40
Urban/Rural Ratios			
Per capita income	2.47		
UHPT/RLPT	2.83		
UHPT/RHPT and ULPT/RLPT	1.98		
ULPT/RHPT	1.38		

Note: LPT = low poverty threshold; HPT = high poverty threshold; U and L designate urban and rural, respectively.

It should be noted that the ratios of our poverty thresholds to average income for urban China (0.28 and 0.4) overlap the range of values for rural China (0.35 and 0.5). In our opinion, there are powerful reasons why these ratios should not be radically different for the rural and urban populations. Poverty thresholds are (nominally) anchored to minimum acceptable levels of food energy consumption. We have chosen a lower level of nutrition for urban China than for the high rural threshold. This can be justified by the higher observed labor force participation rate and a possibly higher intensity of work in rural China than in urban China. But another reason to adopt this relatively unusual step is to narrow somewhat the wide urban–rural differences in poverty thresholds. The reason for the big difference is the far higher unit cost of a kilocalorie of food energy in urban China than in rural China, even when the comparison is between the consumption of the *poorest decile* of urban consumers and the *average* of rural consumers. This could result from a variety of causes: a difference in the relative price of food, a difference in consumer preference, and a difference in constraints on preference that consumers in the two societies face.[14] Although we cannot quantify their relative importance, each of these factors must explain a part of the difference in the unit cost of food energy.

Nevertheless, we must deal with the argument that some of our poverty thresholds imply that rural residents just above poverty would have to double or triple their income to be counted as non-poor if they moved to an urban location. Is this plausible? Certainly a doubling of nominal income by migration would mean some increase in real income; however, it is not implausible to consider a migrant as moving from the category of rural non-poor to that of urban poor, even though migration results in a rise in income at constant purchasing power. Recall our discussion at the beginning of this section of the relative nature of poverty thresholds, which explicitly or implicitly express a society's (changing) standard of what constitutes a minimum acceptable income. A rural-urban migrant in China is moving from a poorer society to a much richer one where the poverty standard is much higher. Indeed, the plausibility of this argument becomes clearer in the context of international migration. A non-poor Chinese migrating to Europe or North America could achieve a substantial increase in real income and yet be counted as poor in the adopted country simply because the cut-off standard of poverty in the latter is far higher than in China.

How do our rural and urban poverty thresholds compare with the estimates used by others? For rural China, the official poverty threshold for 1995 is 540 yuan, or 34.2% of per capita income as estimated by the SSB. This is similar to (slightly lower than) our ratio for the RLPT, and well below that of our RHPT. For urban China, the official poverty threshold for 1994 is, however, a higher proportion of official per capita income (45.3%) than is even our UHPT. The World Bank, by contrast, used a poverty threshold for urban China for 1990 which was only 23% of per capita income as estimated by the SSB, well below even our ULPT. This dismally low threshold was actually 30% below the actual food expenditure of the poorest 5% of urban households in 1990, and 60% below the average aggregate expenditure of the same group as estimated by the SSB! To use such a poverty threshold is to start with the presumption that there is *no* urban poverty.

We take care to provide users of our results with substantial choice. In view of the inevitable arbitrariness that is involved in the determination of poverty thresholds, we have purposely put forward alternative thresholds in order to ascertain what happens to poverty levels and trends when the thresholds are changed. In addition, the use of alternative thresholds enables readers to select the combination of rural and urban thresholds that they find most reasonable. Thus, the combination of the ULPT with the RHPT selects a rural threshold that is only 28% below the urban one. This is probably close to the absolute urban–rural difference in purchasing power of income. Alternatively, one might think that an allowance does need to be made for the difference in average living standards between rural and urban China, but that this should be less than the larger gaps yielded by our thresholds. In this case, the intermediate threshold for rural China might be combined with the low one for urban China.

Consumer Price Indices for Poverty Thresholds

The evidence in Table 2.2 strongly suggests that changes in rural and urban CPIs (henceforth simply "rural and urban CPIs") between 1988 and 1995 understate respective consumer price increases for households at poverty levels. We nevertheless accept the official CPIs as the basic set of deflators to estimate the poverty thresholds for 1988. We then estimate an *adjusted set of CPIs* to deflate the poverty thresholds for 1995 and thus to arrive at alternative sets of poverty thresholds for 1988, as follows.

The CPI is the weighted average of the food CPI (P_f) and the non-food CPI (P_{nf}). For urban China, we use the Industrial Consumer Goods Price Index as the non-food CPI. Next, we estimate the food CPI from the following equation: $0.499P_f + 0.501(206.86) = 227.9$, where 0.499 is the average urban share of consumer expenditure on food, 206.86 is the non-food CPI, and 227.9 is the CPI. This gives us an urban food CPI of 249.02. We then decompose the urban food CPI into CPI for grain and for non-grain food by using the urban grain price index (489.09) and the average share of grain in urban food expenditure (14.7%). Next, we estimate the urban food CPI relevant for the poor by weighting the price indices for grain and non-grain food by their respective weights for the *poorest decile* (19.3% for grain). Finally, we average the urban food CPI for the poor with the non-food CPI, using the expenditure weights of the poorest decile (55% for food). The adjusted urban CPI is 237.15, 9.25 points (or 4.1%) higher than the official one (see Table 4.4).

The adjusted rural index makes a one-stage adjustment by averaging together the food CPI (assumed to be the same as the urban food CPI) and the non-food CPI (assumed to be the same as the Industrial Products Rural Retail Price Index), using the rural consumer expenditure weights at the poverty threshold (60% for food). The adjusted rural CPI is 228.72, 8.6 points (or 3.9%) higher than the official one.

In our view, the adjusted indices represent the minimum upward adjustment of CPIs that one might make from all possible alternatives shown in Table 2.2. On average, they represent roughly 0.5% higher increase in CPI per year than the unadjusted indices. It is also note-

TABLE 4.4. Poverty Thresholds and CPIs (Values in Current Yuan)

Poverty Thresholds	1988		1995	
	Yuan	% of Income	Yuan	% of Income
High				
Rural unadjusted	526	69.2	1,157	50.1
Rural adjusted	506	66.6	1,157	50.1
Urban unadjusted	1,005	54.6	2,291	40.1
Urban adjusted	966	52.4	2,291	40.1
Intermediate				
Rural unadjusted	421	55.4	926	40.1
Rural adjusted	405	53.3	926	40.1
Urban unadjusted	804	43.6	1,833	32.1
Urban adjusted	773	42.0	1,833	32.1
Low				
Rural unadjusted	368	48.4	810	35.1
Rural adjusted	354	46.6	810	35.1
Urban unadjusted	704	38.2	1,604	28.1
Urban adjusted	676	36.7	1,604	28.1

CPIs	1988	1995
Rural CPI		
Unadjusted	100.00	220.09
Adjusted	100.00	228.72
Urban CPI		
Unadjusted	100.00	227.90
Adjusted	100.00	237.15

worthy that the CPI implicit in SSB's own rural poverty thresholds in 1988 and 1995 is 228.8, the same as the adjusted rural CPI estimate in Table 4.4.[15]

There are clear deficiencies in our estimation of the poverty thresholds. One important inadequacy is the neglect of regional differences in cost of living. The reason for this is the absence of available information. SSB's own poverty thresholds suffer from the same deficiency, even though they should have access to information necessary to make adjustment for regional differences. The consequence of this neglect is that our poverty threshold represents somewhat different levels of living for different locations.

A second issue is that income, rather than expenditure, is the variable in terms of which the poverty threshold is defined. It has been argued that expenditure is a better measure of "permanent income" than is current income. A discussion of the validity or otherwise of this argument is operationally irrelevant because distributional data in China are available only for income.

A final point that deserves to be highlighted is that, although the poverty thresholds have been anchored to desirable levels of nutrition in the benchmark year (1995), there is no requirement that in other years households at poverty thresholds would consume the same level of food energy. Indeed, food energy at the constant-real-income poverty threshold must have been higher in 1988 than in 1995 owing to a sharp rise in relative food prices between the two periods. To ensure constant levels of food energy consumption at poverty thresholds in the two years would require a poverty threshold for 1995 that represents a real income higher than does the threshold for 1988. Our poverty thresholds represent constant standards of living in the sense that consumers in 1995 *could* buy the same bundle of food and other goods that they bought in 1988 if they so desired. In reality, however, a typical consumer with constant standard of living (i.e., income with unchanged purchasing power) and unchanged preferences probably purchased substantially less food in 1995 than in 1988 owing to the massive rise in the relative price of food.

3. Estimates of Poverty

Three different indices of poverty—the Head Count (HC) index, the Proportionate Poverty Gap (PPG) index, and the Weighted Poverty Gap (WPG) index—have been estimated. These have been explained in section 1 above.

For 1995, we have three sets of poverty estimates for rural and urban China and each of their provinces, respectively measuring poverty according to the high, intermediate, and low poverty thresholds. For 1988 each of these sets has two variants, one for the unadjusted CPI and the other for the adjusted CPI. Our discussion of poverty will focus on patterns and trends, not levels per se, because the levels are sensitive to poverty thresholds which, as already noted, are in the ultimate analysis matters of arbitrary decisions. The level of any poverty index will be lower for the LPT than for the HPT. But there is no a priori basis to expect that the *trends* for the three indexes will be necessarily the same, different, or related in any particular way.

However, the trend of estimates based on the unadjusted CPI will differ from that based on the adjusted CPI. In particular, the change in any index of poverty between 1988 and 1995 will be less favorable according to the adjusted CPI because it indicates a higher rate of increase in cost of living, and hence a sharper rise in the nominal value of the poverty threshold between the two dates.

Rural Poverty

Tables 4.5, 4.6, 4.7 and 4.8, summarize various indices of poverty for rural China and its nineteen provinces in our sample for 1988 and 1995.[16] We would like to begin the reporting of results by warning again that some of our provincial samples are not large enough to provide estimates that can be accepted with confidence. This problem

TABLE 4.5. Indices of Broad Rural Poverty (Unadjusted High Poverty Threshold)

	Head Count		Proportionate Poverty Gap		Weighted Poverty Gap	
	1988	1995	1988	1995	1988	1995
All China	35.1	28.6	11.5	8.2	5.7	3.5
Gansu	69.7	69.0	23.2	26.4	10.2	13.0
Guizhou	58.3	61.8	20.9	19.1	10.2	8.3
Shanxi	51.9	49.5	17.0	16.3	8.3	7.7
Shaanxi	59.9	58.0	20.7	18.5	10.1	7.8
Yunnan	47.3	45.6	14.0	10.6	5.8	3.7
Hunan	13.1	37.5	3.1	12.0	1.6	5.1
Sichuan	32.5	43.1	9.5	12.1	4.5	5.0
Jiangxi	25.7	27.0	5.9	5.9	2.3	2.2
Anhui	35.6	19.8	10.8	4.9	5.2	1.8
Henan	52.5	20.1	19.0	4.2	9.8	1.6
Hubei	20.3	25.0	4.6	8.6	1.7	4.3
Hebei	29.9	22.7	8.6	6.1	3.7	2.5
Liaoning	27.0	21.9	8.4	5.2	4.3	1.9
Jilin	41.5	18.3	14.6	4.4	8.9	1.7
Shandong	28.3	19.3	8.1	4.6	3.8	2.0
Zhejiang	5.8	4.0	2.3	0.7	1.5	0.3
Jiangsu	27.8	4.7	9.4	1.1	5.2	0.6
Guangdong	4.8	5.2	1.2	1.3	0.6	0.5
Beijing	8.7	1.3	2.8	0.8	1.4	0.5

Note: The Head Count index is the number of persons belonging to households with average income less than the poverty threshold as per cent of all persons. The proportionate poverty gap shows the ratio of the total income gap of all poor persons from the poverty threshold as a percent of the total income needed by the entire population to get to the poverty threshold (poverty threshold times the population). The weighted poverty gap shows the sum of squares of the proportionate income gaps of all the poor divided by the by size of population. In estimating PG and WPG, a lower limit of zero has been set on income.

TABLE 4.6. Indices of Deep Rural Poverty (Unadjusted Intermediate Poverty Threshold)

	Head Count		Proportionate Poverty Gap		Weighted Poverty Gap	
	1988	1995	1988	1995	1988	1995
All China	22.6	17.4	7.2	4.6	3.6	1.9
Gansu	50.5	54.5	13.9	17.3	5.4	7.8
Guizhou	40.6	40.7	13.8	10.9	6.2	4.4
Shanxi	35.1	35.2	10.8	10.0	5.1	4.5
Shaanxi	41.6	41.5	13.1	10.6	6.2	4.0
Yunnan	30.2	24.1	7.6	4.5	3.0	1.5
Hunan	5.7	27.1	1.8	7.0	1.2	2.6
Sichuan	18.6	25.7	5.6	6.6	2.8	2.6
Jiangxi	12.2	11.9	2.7	2.8	1.2	1.1
Anhui	19.6	11.4	6.6	2.3	3.3	0.8
Henan	39.1	8.3	12.4	1.9	6.4	0.8
Hubei	8.4	17.1	2.1	5.7	0.9	2.6
Hebei	16.8	12.6	4.8	3.1	2.1	1.3
Liaoning	16.2	11.0	5.2	2.5	2.9	0.8
Jilin	25.3	7.9	10.3	2.1	6.9	0.9
Shandong	16.7	8.7	4.5	2.5	2.4	1.2
Zhejiang	3.9	1.5	1.6	0.2	1.2	0.2
Jiangsu	16.2	1.3	6.3	0.7	3.7	0.5
Guangdong	2.1	2.9	0.7	0.7	0.4	0.2
Beijing	5.3	1.3	1.9	0.6	0.8	0.3

Note: See note to Table 4.5 for explanation.

is particularly serious in the discussion, later in this chapter, of some of the characteristics of the poor for which the total number of observations is very low for some provinces.

Broad poverty. This term refers to estimates of poverty for the high poverty threshold without any adjustment in CPI. There was a modest decline of 19% in the HC index of rural broad poverty between 1988 and 1995, a period during which rural per capita real income increased by 38%.[17] The estimated number of poor rural inhabitants fell from 289 million to 246 million, a 15% reduction. Had the distribution of rural income in 1995 remained the same as in 1988, the HC index of broad rural poverty would have declined by much more — about 50%.[18]

The proportionate poverty gap, which shows the combined effect of the proportion of population in poverty and the average depth of

TABLE 4.7. Indices of Extreme Rural Poverty (Unadjusted Low Poverty Threshold)

	Head Count		Proportionate Poverty Gap		Weighted Poverty Gap	
	1988	1995	1988	1995	1988	1995
All China	16.9	12.1	5.4	3.1	2.8	1.3
Gansu	37.7	43.9	9.5	12.8	3.4	5.6
Guizhou	34.2	28.5	10.4	7.5	4.4	2.9
Shanxi	26.0	24.3	7.9	7.3	3.8	3.3
Shaanxi	32.1	28.9	9.6	7.0	4.6	2.5
Yunnan	20.6	12.7	5.0	2.6	2.0	0.9
Hunan	3.6	19.2	1.4	4.7	1.0	1.6
Sichuan	13.2	18.5	4.2	4.3	2.2	1.7
Jiangxi	7.2	8.3	1.7	1.8	0.9	0.7
Anhui	15.5	6.4	5.0	1.3	2.5	0.5
Henan	28.6	5.0	9.3	1.2	5.0	0.6
Hubei	6.4	14.1	1.4	4.3	0.6	1.8
Hebei	11.6	7.7	3.4	2.0	1.5	1.0
Liaoning	11.3	7.3	3.9	1.4	2.5	0.5
Jilin	18.5	6.5	8.7	1.4	6.1	0.6
Shandong	11.5	5.9	3.3	1.8	2.0	0.9
Zhejiang	2.6	0.2	1.4	0.2	1.1	0.2
Jiangsu	13.2	1.2	5.1	0.6	3.1	0.5
Guangdong	1.2	2.2	0.5	0.4	0.3	0.2
Beijing	4.6	1.3	1.4	0.5	0.6	0.2

Note: See note to Table 4.5 for explanation.

poverty of the poor, declined by more, 29%. The rate of decline in the distributionally weighted index of poverty was even greater—39%—indicating an improvement in the distribution of income among those below the broad poverty threshold.

The incidence of broad poverty is by and large lower for the provinces with higher per capita income. Spearman's rank correlation coefficient between the provincial rank in head count rural poverty and the provincial rank in per capita rural income is a highly significant −0.69.[19]

The rate of change in broad poverty was not the same everywhere. In five provinces—Jiangsu, Jilin, Henan, Anhui, and Beijing—the HC index of poverty declined rapidly. In another four provinces—Shandong, Liaoning, Hebei, and Zhejiang—there was a moderately rapid decline in the index. In Gansu, Shanxi, Shaanxi, and Yunnan, the rate

TABLE 4.8. Indices of Rural Poverty, Adjusted CPI, 1988 (Poverty Thresholds Based on Adjusted CPI)

	High Poverty Threshold			Intermediate Poverty Threshold			Low Poverty Threshold		
	HC	PPG	WPG	HC	PPG	WPG	HC	PPG	WPG
All China	32.7	10.6	5.2	20.9	6.6	3.4	15.5	4.9	2.6
Gansu	67.1	21.4	9.2	46.6	12.5	4.7	34.3	8.4	3.0
Guizhou	55.3	19.5	9.4	39.1	12.8	5.7	32.4	9.5	4.0
Shanxi	47.4	15.7	7.6	32.9	9.9	4.7	24.1	7.2	3.5
Shaanxi	56.9	19.2	9.3	37.9	12.0	5.7	28.8	8.8	4.2
Yunnan	44.3	12.7	5.2	27.4	6.8	2.7	19.0	4.4	1.8
Hunan	10.7	2.8	1.5	5.1	1.6	1.1	3.1	1.3	1.0
Sichuan	29.5	8.7	4.2	16.4	5.1	2.6	12.4	3.8	2.1
Jiangxi	24.7	5.2	2.0	10.5	2.4	1.1	5.7	1.5	0.8
Anhui	31.8	9.9	4.8	18.8	6.1	3.1	15.1	4.6	2.3
Henan	50.1	17.8	9.1	35.2	11.4	6.0	25.5	8.6	4.7
Hubei	18.5	4.0	1.5	7.1	1.9	0.8	5.8	1.2	0.6
Hebei	27.5	7.8	3.4	15.5	4.3	1.9	10.7	3.1	1.4
Liaoning	24.5	7.7	4.0	15.3	4.8	2.8	10.6	3.7	2.3
Jilin	37.0	13.6	8.4	22.6	9.8	6.6	17.9	8.3	5.9
Shandong	25.6	7.3	3.5	14.3	4.1	2.3	9.8	3.0	1.9
Zhejiang	5.3	2.2	1.4	3.4	1.6	1.2	2.6	1.3	1.1
Jiangsu	25.0	8.7	4.9	14.4	5.9	3.6	12.0	4.9	3.0
Guangdong	4.4	1.1	0.5	2.1	0.6	0.4	1.1	0.5	0.3
Beijing	8.7	2.6	1.3	5.3	1.7	0.7	4.6	1.3	0.5

Note: HC = Head Count index; PPG = Proportionate Poverty Gap index; WPG = Weighted Poverty Gap index. See note to Table 4.5 for further explanation.

of head count poverty reduction was very slow. In six provinces—Guizhou, Hunan, Sichuan, Jiangxi, Hubei, and Guangdong—the HC index of poverty increased, often quite rapidly.

The proportionate poverty gap increased in five provinces (Gansu, Hunan, Sichuan, Hubei, and Guangdong), remained unchanged in Jiangxi, and declined by at least a significant margin in ten provinces (Yunnan, Anhui, Henan, Hebei, Liaoning, Jilin, Shandong, Zhejiang, Jiangsu, and Beijing). In the remaining three provinces (Guizhou, Shanxi, and Shaanxi), the rate of decline in the proportionate poverty gap was small. The weighted poverty gap, incorporating the effect of the distribution of income among the poor, declined in all but four provinces (Gansu, Hunan, Sichuan, and Hubei), in which it rose.

Poverty reduction was by and large positively associated with the growth of income, but there were a few notable exceptions. Guangdong, one of the richest provinces, with the lowest incidence of poverty in 1988, recorded a rise in the first two poverty indices in spite of a very high rate of growth in income. Anhui had a less than average rate of income growth but one of the most rapid rates of reduction in all three indices of poverty. Hebei and Liaoning, both coastal provinces, had well below the average rate of income growth but moderately rapid reduction in broad poverty.

In all the provinces in which broad poverty increased—with the exception of Guangdong—the rate of income growth was well below the average for rural China. All the provinces that experienced a rapid reduction in poverty, with the exception of Anhui, achieved a higher than average growth in income. Of the seven coastal provinces included in the rural survey, poverty declined in six. Guangdong is the only coastal province in which broad poverty increased, although all its broad poverty indices remained low in 1995.

Deep poverty. This term refers to estimates of poverty for the intermediate poverty thresholds, equal to 80% of the high poverty thresholds. There was a more rapid reduction in deep than in broad rural poverty: the overall HC index decreased by 23% while the Proportionate Poverty Gap index declined by 36%. The rate of decline in the distributionally weighted poverty gap was even greater—47%—confirming that there was a significant improvement in income distribution among those whose incomes were well below the high poverty threshold. However, a simulation exercise once again shows that the decline in the HC index of deep rural poverty would have been much higher (approximately 50%) if the distribution of rural income in 1995 had remained the same as in 1988. The broad pattern of deep poverty trends among provinces remains the same as for broad poverty, with some minor changes which can be ascertained by comparing Table 4.6 with Table 4.5.

Extreme poverty. This term refers to estimates of poverty derived by using the lowest poverty threshold we constructed, one equal to 70% of the high poverty threshold. The head count rate of extreme poverty declined by 28%, the greatest decline of the three head count rates (see Table 4.9). The proportionate poverty gap and the weighted poverty gap for the very poor below the low threshold declined by 43% and 54%, respectively. Trends in extreme poverty among the provinces are more favorable than trends in the other kinds of poverty. Guizhou, which showed an increase in head count rates of broad and

TABLE 4.9. Reductions in Rural Poverty Head Count Index
Using Alternative CPIs

Poverty Index	Reduction with Adjusted CPI (%)	Reduction with Official CPI (%)
Broad poverty	13	19
Deep poverty	17	23
Extreme poverty	22	28

deep poverty, registered a decline in the incidence of extreme poverty according to all indices.

Rural poverty estimates based on adjusted CPI. The conversion to constant purchasing power of the poverty thresholds in the estimates reported in Tables 4.5, 4.6, and 4.7 are based on the rate of change in the official CPI between 1988 and 1995. We argued in the previous section that this results in an understatement of the increase in cost of living for those households that are at or below the poverty threshold. We also estimated alternative CPIs which make a minimum allowance for the higher rate of increase in the cost of living of the poor. Table 4.8 shows the estimates of broad, deep, and extreme rural poverty for 1988, based on poverty thresholds which are adjusted by this more realistic alternative CPI.[20] By comparing these indices of poverty with the corresponding estimates for 1995 shown in Tables 4.5, 4.6 and 4.7, we find that the reduction of rural poverty has been significantly slower than is suggested by the results reported above. (This comparison for the HC index only is shown in Table 4.9.) Using the adjusted CPI, the HC index of broad poverty declines by 13%, that for deep poverty by 17% and that for extreme poverty by 22% (as compared to 19%, 23%, and 28% for the respective unadjusted poverty thresholds). Also, four more provinces — Gansu, Shanxi, Shaanxi, and Yunnan — show a rise in broad poverty, causing a majority of provinces to show a rise in broad poverty between 1988 and 1995.

Urban Poverty

Tables 4.10 through 4.14 summarize the indices of poverty for urban China and its provinces for 1988 and 1995. The incidence of urban poverty is much lower than that of rural poverty, an expected outcome of the far higher standard of living in urban China. It is also well below the estimates shown in Table 4.1 (which are based on SSB's grouped

TABLE 4.10. Indices of Urban Broad Poverty (Unadjusted High Poverty Threshold)

	Head Count		Proportionate Poverty Gap		Weighted Poverty Gap	
	1988	1995	1988	1995	1988	1995
All China	8.2	8.0	1.4	2.0	0.4	0.8
Shanxi	24.1	20.7	4.5	5.3	1.3	2.1
Henan	16.0	21.1	2.3	5.8	0.6	2.3
Anhui	13.8	6.9	2.3	1.3	0.6	0.4
Yunnan	7.9	6.1	1.3	0.9	0.4	0.3
Hubei	3.7	5.3	0.4	1.3	0.1	0.8
Sichuan	—	7.3	—	1.8	—	0.7
Liaoning	1.8	5.7	0.2	1.1	0.0	0.3
Gansu	6.3	12.9	1.5	3.4	0.7	1.2
Jiangsu	2.6	1.8	0.4	0.5	0.2	0.2
Beijing	0.0	0.6	0.0	0.1	0.0	0.0
Guangdong	0.6	0.9	0.1	0.2	0.0	0.0

TABLE 4.11. Indices of Urban Deep Poverty (Unadjusted Intermediate Poverty Threshold)

	Head Count		Proportionate Poverty Gap		Weighted Poverty Gap	
	1988	1995	1988	1995	1988	1995
All China	2.7	4.1	0.4	0.9	0.1	0.4
Shanxi	9.1	11.5	1.5	2.8	0.4	1.0
Henan	4.7	12.7	0.6	3.0	0.1	1.1
Anhui	4.6	2.8	0.7	0.4	0.2	0.1
Yunnan	2.4	1.6	0.5	0.3	0.1	0.1
Hubei	0.8	1.7	0.1	0.8	0.0	0.6
Sichuan	—	3.6	—	0.9	—	0.4
Liaoning	0.5	2.5	0.0	0.3	0.0	0.1
Gansu	2.8	7.6	0.8	1.6	0.4	0.5
Jiangsu	0.6	1.2	0.1	0.3	0.1	0.2
Beijing	0.0	0.0	0.0	0.0	0.0	0.0
Guangdong	0.2	0.3	0.0	0.1	0.0	0.0

Note: See note to Table 4.5 for explanation.

TABLE 4.12. Indices of Urban Extreme Poverty (Unadjusted Low Poverty Threshold)

	Head Count		Proportionate Poverty Gap		Weighted Poverty Gap	
	1988	1995	1988	1995	1988	1995
All China	1.3	2.7	0.2	0.6	0.1	0.3
Shanxi	4.9	7.9	0.7	1.8	0.2	0.7
Henan	1.7	9.0	0.2	1.9	0.0	0.7
Anhui	2.1	1.7	0.3	0.2	0.1	0.1
Yunnan	1.6	0.9	0.3	0.2	0.1	0.1
Hubei	0.2	1.6	0.0	0.7	0.0	0.6
Sichuan	—	2.1	—	0.6	—	0.3
Liaoning	0.0	1.2	0.0	0.1	0.0	0.0
Gansu	1.7	4.4	0.6	0.9	0.4	0.3
Jiangsu	0.1	0.8	0.1	0.2	0.1	0.1
Beijing	0.0	0.0	0.0	0.0	0.0	0.0
Guangdong	0.2	0.3	0.0	0.0	0.0	0.0

TABLE 4.13. Indices of Urban Poverty Based on Adjusted CPI, 1988 (Poverty Thresholds Based on Adjusted CPI)

	Broad Poverty			Deep Poverty			Extreme Poverty		
	HC	PPG	WPG	HC	PPG	WPG	HC	PPG	WPG
All China	6.7	1.1	0.3	2.2	0.4	0.1	1.1	0.2	0.1
Shanxi	20.9	3.8	1.1	8.0	1.3	0.3	4.3	0.6	0.1
Henan	12.6	1.8	0.4	3.7	0.4	0.1	1.4	0.2	0.0
Anhui	11.9	1.9	0.5	3.7	0.5	0.2	1.8	0.2	0.1
Yunnan	6.1	1.1	0.3	2.1	0.4	0.1	1.1	0.2	0.1
Hubei	2.4	0.3	0.1	0.7	0.0	0.0	0.1	0.0	0.0
Liaoning	1.3	0.2	0.0	0.2	0.0	0.0	0.0	0.0	0.0
Gansu	5.2	1.3	0.6	2.4	0.7	0.4	1.5	0.5	0.4
Jiangsu	2.0	0.3	0.1	0.5	0.1	0.1	0.1	0.1	0.1
Beijing	0.0	0.0	0.0	0.0	0.0	0.0	0.0	0.0	0.0
Guangdong	0.6	0.1	0.0	0.2	0.0	0.0	0.0	0.0	0.0

Note: HC = Head Count index; PPG = Proportionate Poverty Gap index; WPG = Weighted Poverty Gap index. See note to Table 4.5 for further explanation.

TABLE 4.14. Change in Urban Poverty Head Count Index Using
Alternative CPIs

Head Count Index	Change with Adjusted CPI (%)	Change with Official CPI (%)
Broad poverty	+19.4	−0.2
Deep poverty	+86.4	+51.9
Extreme poverty	+145.5	+107.7

data), especially for 1988.[21] As in rural China, there is a great deal of variability in the incidence of urban poverty among provinces. It is also generally inversely related to the level of provincial income. For 1995, Spearman's rank correlation coefficient between the provincial rank in per capita income and the provincial rank in the incidence of head count poverty was a significant −0.77.

Broad poverty estimates based on unadjusted CPI. There was virtually no change in the proportion of urban population in broad poverty between 1988 and 1995, a period which saw unprecedented overall growth of urban China and a rise of 36% in real per capita disposable urban household income. This is true even when an obviously understated CPI is used to adjust the poverty threshold. Since urban population increased over this period, the estimated number of urban residents in poverty rose from 23.5 million in 1988 to 28.1 million in 1995—an increase of 20%!

A simulation exercise which assumes an unchanged distribution of income between 1988 and 1995 and the actual growth in urban personal income shows that the proportion of urban population in broad poverty would have declined to less than 1% by the latter year; that is, urban poverty should have been virtually eliminated. Instead, an adverse change in the distribution of income led to stagnation in the proportion—and a much larger absolute number—of the urban population in broad poverty.

In reality, the trend was even worse than this. The use of a more realistic consumer price index to deflate the growth of urban income over the period results in a 19% rise in the proportion of the urban population in broad poverty (shown by comparing Table 4.13 with Table 4.10).

Furthermore, as noted in Chapter 1, our survey drew its sample from registered urban households, thereby ignoring the "floating migrants," whose number has increased over time. Their circumstances are many and varied, and generalizations about their average incomes are therefore precarious, although these must in general be superior to average incomes in the migrants' rural places of origin. Nevertheless, it is highly probable that the incidence of poverty is greater among the migrants than among the registered urban residents. Had migrants been included in the estimates, therefore, the increase in the incidence of urban poverty would probably have been substantially higher.

Another important aspect of the trend in urban broad poverty is that the average income shortfall of the urban poor increased sharply, resulting in a significant rise in the proportionate poverty gap index. Furthermore, the distributionally weighted poverty gap also increased rather sharply, indicating a worsening of the distribution of income among the urban poor.

As in the case of rural China, the change in the incidence of urban broad poverty was not uniform everywhere. In Anhui, it declined rapidly. Again as in the case of the trend in rural poverty, Anhui is the outlier, with a rate of growth in urban income which was significantly lower than average and a rate of reduction in broad poverty which was substantially higher than average. Jiangsu, a coastal province, achieved a higher than average growth in per capita urban income. However, the broad poverty outcome it experienced is mixed: it registered a decline in the HC index of broad poverty, but a rise in the PPG index. In Shanxi and Yunnan, the proportion of urban population in broad poverty declined moderately; these provinces also achieved less than average growth in per capita urban income. In six provinces—Gansu, Hubei, Henan, Liaoning, Beijing, and Guangdong—there was an increase in the proportion of urban population in poverty. The result is not unexpected for Gansu, Hubei, and Henan, which are all poor provinces with less than average growth in urban income during the period under review. For Liaoning, Beijing, and Guangdong, however, the outcome is rather unexpected in view of their high income and higher than average growth in income during the period. We have no direct information about the trend in urban broad poverty in the remaining province, Sichuan, which was not part of the 1988 urban survey.

With the exception of Anhui and Yunnan, the proportionate poverty gap increased everywhere. Except for these two provinces, the weighted poverty gap also increased or remained unchanged everywhere.

Deep urban poverty with unadjusted CPI. Once a lower poverty threshold—80% of the high poverty threshold—is used, the *levels* of the estimated indices of poverty fall substantially. But the rising trend becomes more accentuated: the HC index for urban China as a whole registers an increase of more than 50%, while the proportionate poverty gap more than doubles, and the weighted poverty gap increases even faster. In urban China, deep poverty grew much faster than did the more moderate kind. Anhui and Yunnan are the only provinces that experienced a reduction in deep poverty; it increased in every other province for which estimates are available.

Urban extreme poverty based on unadjusted CPI. When we use an even lower poverty threshold—70% of the high threshold—the *levels* of urban poverty diminish to very low rates. The rising *trend* in poverty, however, becomes very rapid. The HC index more than doubles, while the proportionate poverty gap and weighted poverty gap treble.

Urban poverty estimates based on adjusted CPI. Once we use the more realistic estimates of urban CPI to deflate poverty thresholds, an even more dismal trend in urban poverty emerges. This is shown (for the HC index only) in Table 4.14, derived by comparing the estimates for 1988 in Table 4.13 with the corresponding estimates for 1995 shown in tables 4.10, 4.11, and 4.12. The HC index of broad poverty increases by almost one-fifth, and the proportionate broad poverty gap increases by more than four-fifths. The weighted poverty gap more than doubles. The corresponding indices for deep and extreme poverty increase at even faster rates.

4. Summary of Findings and Comparison with Others' Results

Summary of Poverty Trends

There was some reduction in the incidence of rural poverty, but its rate of reduction was far less than it would have been had the growth in rural income inequality been avoided. In addition, the magnitude of reduction in rural poverty looks much less impressive when the official CPI is replaced by a somewhat more realistic CPI, the situation depicted in Figure 4.1. A redeeming feature of this performance is that the reduction in poverty was greater for the more severe kinds of poverty, as measured both by progressively lower poverty thresholds and by indices that go beyond mere head counts to gauge the average and distributionally weighted poverty gaps. This indicates that, although the distribution of overall rural income worsened, the distribution of income improved somewhat *among the poor*, especially the population in severe poverty. Rural poverty increased in many provinces, including the populous provinces in the heartland of China.

There has been an increase in the incidence of urban poverty. This is shown in Figure 4.2, which illustrates that the rate of increase was faster for more extreme kinds of poverty. Indicators for all kinds of

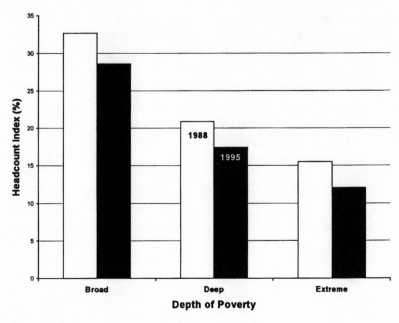

Figure 4.1. Rural Poverty Rates, 1988 and 1995.

poverty show strongly upward trends when the more reasonable CPI is used (as shown in Fig. 4.2) to deflate poverty thresholds. The rising trend in urban poverty is nearly universal among the provinces for which we have estimates.

How Do these Results Compare with Alternative Estimates?

Except for some estimates made by Chinese scholars and officials — mostly unpublished at the time we are writing — there are no estimates of poverty known to us for the *exact* period covered by this study. Nonetheless, it is clear that the results of this study are significantly different from official estimates and estimates made by independent researchers on the basis of official data. Official estimates of rural poverty claim a faster reduction in poverty than our estimates do, while unofficial estimates based on official data (e.g., those in Khan, 1996) suggest a slower reduction between the mid-1980s and 1994.[22] As noted earlier, a World Bank study covering the period up to 1990 finds no trend in the HC index of rural poverty after 1984. Subsequent World Bank estimates have the *total* incidence of poverty declining, on the basis of "national poverty lines," from 8.4% in 1987 to 8.1% in 1993, 6.9% in 1994, and below 6% in 1995.[23]

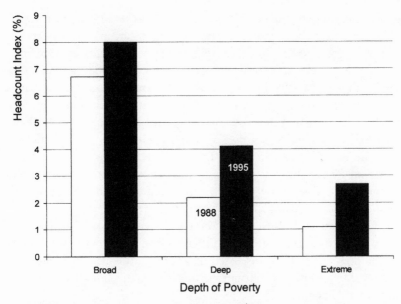

Figure 4.2. Urban Poverty Rates, 1988 and 1995. (The poverty rates shown for 1988 are based on the adjusted CPI.)

Assuming these numbers represent rural poverty (consistent with the view expressed in World Bank publications that poverty in China is almost entirely a rural phenomenon), they yield a total reduction in the HC index of about 30% between 1987 and 1995. This is well above our estimated reduction of 18.5% for unadjusted broad poverty, 12.5% for adjusted broad poverty, and 21.9% for adjusted extreme poverty.

Estimates of urban poverty based on official data suggest a significant reduction in poverty between the late 1980s and the mid-1990s (for example, Khan, 1996, shows a reduction of more than 20% between 1989 and 1994; estimates for 1988 and 1995 are not available).

Studies made by Chinese scholars—presumably based on official data—often arrive at substantially different results. An example is an unpublished study of rural poverty by Xian Zude and Sheng Laiyun, the only study known to us that covers the years 1988 and 1995.[24] According to their estimates, the HC index of rural poverty declined by nearly one-half between 1988 and 1995. A study of urban poverty for the 1990s, by Ren Caifang and Chen Xiaojie, shows no clear trend.[25]

These two studies indicate trends in poverty that are different from those identified by studies made by foreign scholars but also based on official Chinese data. The reason for the discrepancy is easy to ascertain:

it is due entirely to the use by the Chinese scholars of poverty thresholds that cannot be regarded as representing an income with unchanged purchasing power over time. The rural poverty study by Xian and Sheng uses poverty thresholds of 341 yuan for 1988 and 502 yuan for 1995, implying a 47% increase in the CPI for the poor. As we have seen, even the understated official CPI for rural China shows an increase of more than 120% over the same period.[26] The study of urban poverty by Ren and Chen uses an implicit CPI that is much higher than the actual increase in the CPI.[27] It is therefore not surprising that Xian and Sheng show a much faster reduction in rural poverty, and that Ren and Chen show a much slower reduction in urban poverty than other studies *based on official data*.

Our point is, however, that the trends based on official data are (or would be) also substantially different from the trends established by the present study. As discussed in section 1, this is true because of the incomplete income accounting underlying the official household surveys in China.

Appendix: Deriving the Poverty Thresholds

Rural Poverty Threshold

The first step in deriving our poverty thresholds is to estimate the average annual cost of a kilocalorie of food per day. Information on eight broad categories of food consumption are given by the SSB; these provide a daily consumption of 2,066 kilocalories per capita per day. (Even this estimate is subject to uncertainty, because units of consumption data are not always unambiguous, and for some categories of food it is hard to judge the appropriateness of international data on nutrition content that have to be used for want of corresponding Chinese data.) From a detailed 1993/1994 survey for Cambodia (see Cambodia, 1995), a country with a food consumption pattern that is broadly similar to China's, we estimate that these eight categories of food provide 87% of total food energy. On this assumption, the average daily kilocalories consumed by a rural Chinese person in 1995 totaled 2,375. We accept this figure as a reasonable estimate of the average value of food energy consumption in rural China. The SSB data on rural household expenditure do not provide separate information for different income groups; only average values are available (see SSB, 1996). Using per capita rural expenditure on food from SSB (1996), and the above estimate of average kilocalories of food energy consumption, we get the unit cost of a kilocalorie *per day* (i.e., a total of 365 kilocalories) to be 0.323 yuan. We assume this average cost to apply to persons at the high poverty threshold (HPT). For a daily requirement of 2,150 kilocalories per capita, this gives a *food* poverty threshold of 695 yuan. The SSB estimates that 58.6% of expenditure of an average rural consumer was on food. We do not know what it would be for our estimate of rural income, which is substantially higher than the SSB estimate, but we note that our higher estimate of income is partly due to a higher valuation of the consumption of self-produced food. We arbitrarily take 60% as the fraction of income spent on food for our HPT, which thus works out to 1,159 yuan.

Alternatively, for the low poverty threshold (LPT), we adopt the same caloric standard as we use for the urban poverty threshold— 2,100 kilocalories. Moreover, for the LPT we also assume that the unit cost of food energy paid by people at the poverty threshold and below was 80% of the unit cost for the average rural consumer, or 0.258 yuan. For a daily requirement of 2,100 kilocalories per capita, this gives a *food* poverty threshold of 542 yuan. A study of consumption patterns of rural households at the poverty threshold in 1988 indicated that 68% of income was spent on food. We settle here for roughly two-thirds—67%—as the proportion of expenditure on food for an average household at the poverty threshold for our LPT group. This yields a low poverty threshold of 809 yuan, which we round up to 810.

The low threshold is equal to 70% of the high one. In order to evaluate the sensitivity of trends in various measures of poverty to the exact threshold chosen, we also specify an *intermediate poverty threshold* between the low and high ones and equal to 80% of the latter. This intermediate threshold works out to be 926 yuan.

Urban Poverty Threshold

The method of deriving the urban poverty threshold is similar to that used for the rural. However, unlike in the rural case, data are available for urban population quintiles and the poorest deciles; therefore, we initially construct only one threshold, based on the parameters for the poorest decile. Then the intermediate and low poverty thresholds for the urban population are fixed simply by taking 80% and 70%, re-spectively, of the estimated standard threshold. The 25 items of food consumption reported by the SSB for the poorest decile of urban con-sumers account for 1,612 kilocalories per person per day. Using the ratio of food energy supplied by these items to the total food energy from the detailed information available from the Cambodian survey (79%), we arrive at a daily per capita consumption of 2,041 kcalories, which seems to be roughly the right order of magnitude for food energy consumption of the *poorest* decile of the urban Chinese. Given the annual expenditure on food for this decile group from SSB sources, we estimate the unit cost of supplying a kilocalorie per day for a year to be 0.60 yuan. Using a daily food energy requirement of 2,100 kcalories, this gives a food poverty threshold of 1,260 yuan. For the poorest decile group, food accounted for 59.5% of expenditure, according to SSB data. Our definition of urban income catches more non-food components than food components that are missing in the SSB definition; thus, it should be a lower proportion of income/expenditure than is the case for SSB data. We use a ratio of 55% which gets us an urban poverty threshold of 2,291 yuan.

5

Gender, Health, and Education
• •

Human Development Dimensions of Inequality

1. Introduction: The Human Development Index

It is now time to discuss some broader aspects of distribution, with respect to both subjects and objects of distribution. Examined over the global population, income is far from perfectly correlated with other aspects of human well-being, such as longevity, health, education, and a clean natural environment. The concept of "sustainable human development" (SHD), promoted by the United Nations Development Programme (UNDP), was designed to examine directly the impact of economic growth (or its absence) on the human capabilities embodied in these and other important aspects of well-being. Inevitably, a new index emerged: UNDP's Human Development Index (HDI), which encompasses the most easily quantified and measured factors that contribute to SHD—longevity, educational status, and income. Special indices were also developed to measure other factors not included in HDI, such as the empowerment of women and the extent of poverty. Still others, such as human freedom and environmental health, have not yet been subject to convincing quantification.

We cannot here investigate all the myriad issues that affect the level of sustainable human development. However, our income surveys yielded data worth reporting that throw light on some of these issues. In this chapter, we deal with two in particular: the status of women and the existence of gender bias; and the distribution of health care. In the context of the first, we also deal with some education issues. These investigations yield insights into aspects of China's economic and social development beyond those that arise from examination of income alone. First, however, we examine the link between the distribution over China's provinces of measured human development—the

81

HDI—and that of income. At issue is this question: How good a proxy for human development at the province level is provincial per capita income?

2. Human Development

In Chapter 3, section 6, we showed that regional inequalities in income distribution grew substantially between 1988 and 1995. We will now investigate whether a similar trend holds for "human development," the concept used by the United Nations to indicate improvements in people's capabilities, and represented in simplified form in the Human Development Index (HDI) published annually for member countries in the *Human Development Report* (HDR).[1]

The HDI was developed by the UNDP to provide a relatively simple measure of human development status, using data that are available for most countries. It consists of an average of three measures: income, longevity, and education.[2] For China's provinces, this index has been calculated for the first time by Li Shi of the Institute of Economics, Chinese Academy of Social Sciences, for 1995, using the official provincial GDP data. Li's estimates can be found in the *China National Human Development Report*,[3] and are reproduced in the appendix to this chapter.

These estimates reveal a correlation between China's provincial HDI ranks and the provincial GDP index ranks that is much closer (rank correlation coefficient is 0.96) than the corresponding correlation reported in the global Human Development Report between national HDI and GDP ranks. Among all provinces, only in little Qinghai, with fewer than 5 million inhabitants, is there a significant difference in rank (greater than three places) between HDI and GDP.

Provincial HDI values were also computed for 1990, and the changes in these values between 1990 and 1995 are shown in the last column of the table given in the Appendix to Chapter 5. These numbers indicate that there has been substantial variation in provincial HDI growth among China's provinces. In general, provinces with higher HDI scores also increased them faster from 1988 to 1995. All five of the high-growth provinces (with HDI growth above 10 points) are situated in coastal areas. Most of the low-growth provinces are poor provinces from western interior regions. Evidently, in China regional differentiation in human development, as measured by HDI, closely follows differentiation by income. Regression analysis indicates that, consistent with the close correlation of per capita GDP with HDI, the difference in the per capita GDP index between 1990 and 1995 explains most of the difference in HDI between the two years.[4]

Taking advantage of our detailed data sets, we recalculated the provincial Human Development Index for the ten provinces for which both urban and rural data are available for both 1988 and 1995. This permits us to use personal disposable income, which is more appropriate than GDP per capita as the income component of the HDI. We also calculated a distribution weighted HDI, which discounts the income component as the inequality of its distribution rises. The results are shown in the two panels of Table 5.1, where the provinces are listed in descending order by 1988 HDI value.

For the ten provinces under consideration, the distribution weighted version of the HDI does not differ significantly from the GDP-based one. Nor does it differ much from the simple unweighted version, especially in 1988. In 1995, distribution weighting breaks a three-way tie for fifth place between Shanxi, Hubei, and Henan and creates a tie for last place between Gansu and Yunnan. The main change between the two years is the exchange of ranks between Liaoning and Jiangsu. These two provinces are respectively emblematic of the old state-controlled economy and the post-reform market-oriented one. Liaoning was the heavy industrial center for the past Soviet-style industrialization program and has had great difficulty adapting to the different demands of the reform era. Its income index grew by "only" one-third between 1988 and 1995, compared to a jump of over 100%

TABLE 5.1a. 1988 and 1995 Provincial Human Development Indices for Ten Provinces, Unweighted Provincial HDIs

	1988 per Capita Income Index	1990 Life Exp. Index	1990 Educ Index	1988 HDI	1995 per Capita Income Index	1995 Educ. Index	1995 HDI	Change in HDI, 1988–1995
Beijing	0.49	0.81	0.82	0.71	0.78	0.86	0.82	0.11
Guangdong	0.41	0.80	0.75	0.65	0.74	0.79	0.78	0.12
Liaoning	0.30	0.76	.078	0.61	0.40	0.80	0.65	0.04
Jiangsu	0.27	0.79	.070	0.59	0.56	0.77	0.71	0.12
Shanxi	0.08	0.74	0.75	0.56	0.21	0.79	0.58	0.02
Hubei	0.23	0.71	0.68	0.54	0.29	0.73	0.58	0.04
Henan	.015	0.75	0.67	0.52	0.24	0.74	0.58	0.05
Anhui	.018	.075	0.60	0.51	0.25	0.72	0.57	0.06
Gansu	.016	0.71	0.57	0.48	0.20	0.62	0.51	0.03
Yunnan	.018	.065	0.58	0.47	0.20	0.64	0.50	0.03

TABLE 5.1b. 1988 and 1995 Provincial Human Development Indices for Ten Provinces, Distribution Weighted Provincial HDIs

	1988 Distrib. Weighted Prov. Income Index	1988 Distrib. Weighted HDI	1995 Distrib. Weighted Prov. Income Index	1995 Distrib. Weighted HDI	Change in HDIs, 1988–1995
Beijing	0.37	0.67	0.61	0.76	0.09
Guangdong	0.29	0.61	0.46	0.68	0.07
Liaoning	0.23	0.59	0.26	0.61	0.02
Jiangsu	0.18	0.56	0.36	0.64	0.08
Shanxi	0.12	0.54	0.17	0.57	0.03
Hubei	0.17	0.52	0.20	0.55	0.02
Henan	0.10	0.51	0.13	0.54	0.03
Anhui	0.13	0.49	0.16	0.54	0.05
Gansu	0.12	0.47	0.10	0.48	0.01
Yunnan	0.13	0.45	0.14	0.48	0.02

Note: Distribution weighting is accomplished by multiplying household per capita income by $(1-G)$, where G is the Gini ratio. This was done separately for urban and rural per capita incomes, using the estimated Gini ratios for each component; the two components were then added together, using the 1990 shares of agricultural and non-agricultural populations as weights.

in that of Jiangsu. Liaoning's distribution weighted income index advanced by only 13%, less than half the proportional increase in the unweighted index; the reason was a sharp increase in urban inequality in a province that is highly urbanized. Jiangsu, on the other hand, has been a center of rapid township and village enterprise (TVE) development. Although its education index also grew more rapidly than Liaoning's, the chief basis for its advance in the provincial HDI rank list was its phenomenal income growth, from a position 3 points below that of Liaoning in 1988 to one 16 points (40%) above it in 1995.

Thus, all estimates of provincial HDIs yield the same result: the more economically developed provinces have achieved a higher human development level as well. This close correlation is important to note. The considerable divergence internationally between the GDP and HDI ranks of countries, as reported in the various global *Human Development Reports,* points up the existence of unexploited potential for improvements in human development at given levels of economic development. Is this not true for the regions of China? Such a simple conclusion would be unwarranted, because it is *rank* correlation that is under consideration here: even if a perfect rank correlation of HDI and GDP were maintained, it would still be possible, through a more redistributive development strategy, to weaken the link between economic growth and human development by improving the human development performance of the poorer provinces and thus reducing the *range* of the distribution of HDI values. China's government budget commands an unusually low share of GDP for public use — about 12%, compared to 17% for India and over 30% for the United States. If government were able to make use of a reasonably larger share of GDP, in line with international experience, to achieve more equal per capita spending on health and education among the provinces, for instance, the HDI numbers of poor provinces would come closer to those of rich, even if the rank order remained unchanged.[5]

Another way to accomplish this would be to reduce the urban bias in social policy. As we have seen (Chap. 3), urban-rural income disparity is the dominant source of overall income inequality in China. One reason for income differences among provinces is differences in their urbanization rates. The more advanced coastal provinces are the more urbanized ones; the backward provinces of the west are the least urbanized. A strategy that began spreading to the rural population resources and benefits heretofore available only to urban residents would tend to reduce interprovincial variation in human development. Rural-urban migration, which has become very large in scale since the 1980s, may well be contributing to this result by making income from urban employment opportunities available in remote, poor villages.

Thus, the close rank correlation between HDI and income, though it implies that economic and human development are closely related in China, does *not* imply that improvements in human development status among China's poorer provinces must await fundamental changes in their economies. Indeed, international development experience suggests that the lines of causation may run the other way, and that the best way to bring about fundamental economic changes in poorer regions is to improve the quality of the human beings living there.

3. Gender Inequality

Gender equality is an essential component of social development, albeit one not encompassed by the HDI. UNDP has developed special indices dedicated to this issue, notably the Gender Empowerment Measure and the Gender-Related Development Index.[6] These indices require data not readily available at the regional level for China, and we do not attempt to construct them here. Our discussion is couched in more general terms.

Gender equality and full participation of women in the social labor force have long been part of public policy in China (UNICEF, 1995). In the public sector, women have benefited from labor protection laws, including maternity leave, and China officially espouses the principle of equal pay for equal work. Legal protection for women has continued to advance; in recent years, the Law on Protection of Women's Rights and Interests (1992) provides for "equal rights with men in all aspects of political, economic, cultural, social and family life" (UNICEF, 1995).

Sex Ratios and Male Preference

Although the latest official statistics indicate that the life expectancy of women (73 years) considerably exceeds that of men (68.7 years), some other demographic indicators attest to disadvantages still borne by women. The most dramatic is the sex ratio. According to the 1995 1% sample population survey, the overall female–male ratio for China was about 0.96, significantly below the ratio of well over 1.0 that would hold if both sexes received equal care.[7] The 1994 national population sample survey revealed a sex ratio at birth in that year of 116.3 males to 100 females, substantially higher than the expected ratio (State Statistical Bureau, 1995).[8] In our 1988 rural sample, there were 127 boys per 100 girls age one or below; in the 1995 rural sample, this ratio was 119 to 100 (Table 5.2).[9] Moreover, female infants have had higher mortality rates than male infants in recent years. The 1990 census showed that female infants had an average mortality rate of 37 per 1,000 live births, as against 32 for male infants—the opposite of what is expected.[10] This disadvantage for infant girls is particularly marked in specific provinces, such as Jiangxi, Guangxi, Fujian, and Gansu (UNICEF, 1995).[11]

These statistics reveal the survival of strong male preference in large parts of rural China. Such attitudes have weakened greatly in the cities and towns, however: the three province-level municipalities (Beijing, Shanghai, and Tianjin), for instance, all have the expected small excess of male mortality over female at birth. Nevertheless, our data show a ratio of boys to girls one year and below of 107.8 to 100, and a zero

TABLE 5.2. Rural Sex Ratio, Children Age 0 to 5, 1995

Age	1988 Ratio: Males to Females	1995 Ratio: Males to Females
0 to 1	1.27	1.19
0 to 5	1.13	1.26

to five years sex ratio of 109.6 to 100, which suggests that some male preference persists in urban areas. More than just traditional attitudes are involved: in rural China, where very few people have pensions of any kind or health insurance, parents are dependent upon their children for care in old age. In practice, this means their sons, since in the majority culture daughters marry out of the village and family and become responsible for their husbands' parents. Therefore, from the individual's viewpoint, preference for sons flows rationally from the need for old age security. This has not been true to the same degree in urban China, where most residents in the past were state sector employees covered by relatively generous pensions, there was a very high labor force participation rate, and women had a relatively high opportunity cost of childbearing and childcare. However, the disappearance of the system of guaranteed lifetime employment, the rapid decay of the former enterprise-based pension and other social welfare systems in recent years, and the slowness with which new systems are being put in place may well be leading city dwellers to conclude that they must fall back on family ties for security in old age—a conclusion that would both threaten the decline in fertility rates and strengthen dormant male preference.

Access to Education

The decentralization of China's fiscal system that has occurred during the transition period has made localities increasingly dependent on their own resource bases to finance current and capital expenditures (see Chap. 7). Especially in poorer rural areas, local governments have had to resort to imposing surtaxes and charging a variety of user fees for access to public services, including primary education. A result has been to make education so expensive that some rural residents have kept their children out of school, and girls are more likely to suffer in this way than boys. The State Education Commission found in a 1995 survey that about half of girls not attending school were kept out because their parents could not afford to send them (UNDP, 1999a).

Our 1995 rural data show that the school enrollment rate for boys from 6 to 16 years of age was 84%, and for girls it was 80.6%. For children from 6 to 12 years of age, the enrollment rates were 84% for boys and 82% for girls. There is thus some evidence of a small disadvantage for girls in access to schooling, especially at the middle school level. All the reported rates were well below officially reported national rates of school enrollment.[12] With respect to educational attainment of adults, we find that men over 15 years of age have an average of 6.6 years of schooling, about 36% more than the average of 4.87 years reported by women.

Treatment of Girls within the Household

Our surveys were not designed to investigate the question of unequal intrahousehold distribution of income, care, attention, food, and other goods that would shed light on the issue of male preference or, to put it negatively, discrimination against girls. Our measure of household per capita income is derived by simply dividing household income by household size and averaging the result over all households. It thus assumes equal distribution of household income among all members.

However, it is possible to draw inferences about intrahousehold distribution, and in particular about prejudicial treatment of girls, indirectly from data about expenditure patterns in households of different composition and leadership. This has been done, using the same data set, by Lina Song (1998), who finds that the presence of young sons is associated with as much as 50% more spending on health care than is the presence of young daughters. This difference is too great to be explained by the somewhat greater fragility of infant boys relative to infant girls, and it suggests that the practice of differentially poor care for the latter might be rather widespread. The presence of sons also leads to a larger reduction in household spending on cigarettes and alcohol than does that of young daughters. Together with the unbalanced sex ratio of young children reported above, this evidence points to the persistence of anti-daughter bias in rural China.

Women in the Labor Force

Women are present in virtually all parts of the labor force. About two-thirds of urban women in China work outside the home, as do more than three-quarters of rural women. Nevertheless, Chinese women do not participate fully and equally with men in economic, political, and social life. Women constitute a very small percentage of senior government officials at all levels, from the center to the township, and they are generally underrepresented in the political arena and in higher managerial positions (UNDP, 1999a). On the other hand, women are probably overrepresented in jobs requiring heavy labor. Our own evidence on these questions is presented below.

The rural female labor force numbered 209.5 million in 1995, or 46.6% of the total rural labor force. In 1996, 54 million rural women worked in township and village enterprises (TVEs), or 41.4% of TVE employment. Although many rural women have taken non-agricultural jobs or joined the flow of migrants seeking work in the towns, surveys have found that a smaller proportion of the female rural labor force (20.7%) than of the male (42.6%) have done so. Our rural survey results are consistent with these findings: of 2,288 respondents who were reported to have left the household for more than a month to work or look for work in 1995, 70% were men. Accordingly, there has been a "feminization of agriculture" in which women have been left to do an increasing share of the farm work. The 1990 national census found that, while women comprised 48% of farm workers nationally, their share was over 50% in developed areas such as Beijing, Shanghai, Jiangsu, and Shandong (UNDP, 1999a; UNICEF 1995). Since then, according to the Women's Federation, women may have come to constitute over half of the agricultural workforce nationally (UNDP, 1999a).

We reported in Griffin and Zhao (1993) that one reason rural women had lower incomes in 1988 was that they were underrepresented in off-farm wage employment, the principal source of higher incomes in the countryside. This remains true in 1995, as Table 5.3 shows. There has been virtually no change in women's share of wage employment (about one-third), and the wages earned in such employment have, if anything, fallen relative to men's. This underrepresentation carries over to retirement status: fewer women are formally retired and receiving pensions.

In 1988, rural women were underrepresented in higher-paid occupations and those requiring more skill and education. The same remains true in 1995, but some gains and some losses have been made in the interim (Table 5.4). Women have increased their representation among Communist Party or government officials from 15% to 23%, and among professional or technical workers from 15% to 29%. Among unskilled workers—a privileged category in the countryside, where wage employment is associated with higher than average income—women have increased their representation from 25% to 41%.

TABLE 5.3. Women's Share of Off-Farm Employment and Wages, 1988 and 1995

	1988	1995
Employed outside household	0.32	0.33
Basic wage for off-farm jobs (ratio: women/men)	0.81	0.76

TABLE 5.4. Shares of Women and Men in Various Rural Occupations, 1988 and 1995 (Percent of Total Employment)

Occupational Category	1988		1995	
	Men	Women	Men	Women
Farmer	49	51	47	53
Unskilled worker	75	25	59	41
Skilled worker	NA	NA	86	14
Professional or technical worker	85	15	71	29
Owner or manager of enterprise	74	26	92	08
Village cadre	94	06	88	12
Official of Party or government office or institution	85	15	77	23
Temporary or contract worker	68	32	65	35
Non-farm individual enterprise	79	21	68	32

Their share of individual (private) enterprises has also grown. On the other hand, at the top of the occupational hierarchy—owner or manager of an enterprise—women have apparently suffered a sharp decline, from 26% in the 1988 sample to only 8% in 1995; their predominance in farm work increased slightly, as was suggested by our discussion of migration.

In the towns and cities, too, women are handicapped by the "triple burden": most work outside the home but are also primarily responsible for child and elder care and housework. In 1995, there were 57.5 million female "workers and staff members" (zhigong), mostly in towns and cities, where they constituted 38.6% of employment in the formal economy. A majority of these women—39.57 million—were employed in the state sector, where they made up 36.1% of employees.

Figure 5.1 shows women's share of employment in various kinds of urban jobs in 1995. They make up a majority of the work force among office workers, unskilled workers, and "other." They exceed their overall share of urban employment among owners of private or individual enterprises, professional workers, and skilled workers. They are badly underrepresented in top managerial positions, such as head of institution and division head.

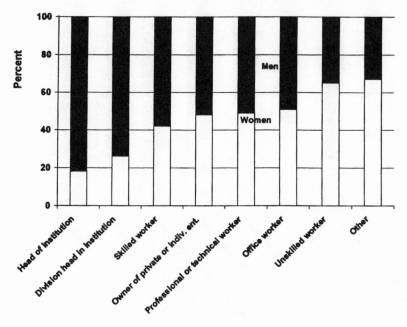

Figure 5.1. Representation in Various Occupations, by Gender

Since women make up about half of urban professional and technical workers, how are they distributed in the hierarchy within these ranks? Figure 5.2 shows them to be underrepresented at the higher levels and in administrative positions (high professional title, cadres at all levels)[13] and concentrated in middle- and lower-level professional and technical categories.

Earnings for urban women also tend to be below those for men. Table 5.5 presents the 1995 survey findings on average incomes of various job categories. For most categories, women received significantly less than men. Their relative deficit was particularly great in the case of overtime pay, "waiting for job" allowance, income from postretirement job, income from second job, individual proprietor's income, and pensions. The last has been a sore point with Chinese women; female workers have had to retire from state jobs at age 50, compared to 55 for men, and female cadres at 55, compared to 60 for men. Since the size of a person's pension depends on the number of years worked, women are at an obvious disadvantage. Men can start working at 20 (worker) or 25 (cadre) years of age and achieve a maximum pension, whereas women would have to begin work at 15 or

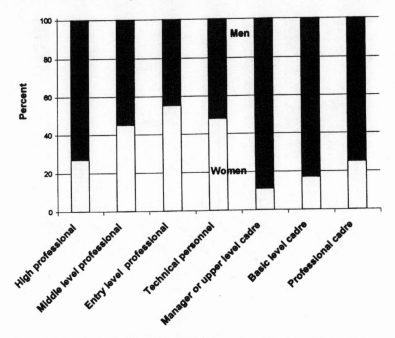

Figure 5.2. Shares by Gender of Professional and Technical Jobs, Urban China, 1995

20 to do so, which in turn would limit their educational opportunities.[14]

There are several possible causes of these differentials, other than discrimination in hiring and firing (of which there is ample qualitative evidence). One such cause is differential educational attainment. Women make up a large majority of those still illiterate and generally receive less education than men; in our sample, the deficit in years is about 8% in the cities and 25% in the countryside (see Table 5.6). Another reason for lower earnings, as we have seen, is that women have been compelled to retire earlier than men and are thus less well represented in senior ranks of their occupations.

Moreover, with their "triple burden" of child and elder care and house work, women are in a weaker position to exploit opportunities for second jobs. One of the surprises of the 1995 survey was the sharp decline in numbers and proportion of people reporting second jobs in the rural areas (Table 5.7). Whereas 30% of rural men and 25% of rural women had reported second jobs in 1988, these figures had fallen to 5% and 2%, respectively, in 1995. We can only speculate at this point about the reasons for this decline. It is possible that in the whole-

TABLE 5.5. Urban Income by Job Category and Sex, 1995

	Women	Men	Ratio: Women/Men
Annual gross income	5,478	6,888	0.80
Wages	50	6,191	0.83
"Waiting for job" allowance		1,137	0.76
Bonuses	63	1,327	0.88
Subsidies and allowances	65	1,304	0.89
Housing subsidy	125	144	0.87
Medical subsidy	144	164	0.88
Child care subsidy	148	168	0.88
Regional subsidies	369	375	0.98
Overtime wages	194	264	0.73
Special circumstance wages	475	495	0.96
Other income from work unit	513	561	0.91
Hardship allowance	341	399	0.85
Individual proprietor's net income*	4,551	5,996	0.76
Income of employees of individual enterprise	4,114	4,750	0.87
Income of re-employed retired worker	2,064	2,751	0.75
Other income from labor	721	1,002	0.72
Income from second job	1,352	2,702	0.50
Property income	593	720	0.82
Interest	499	589	0.85
Dividends	588	910	0.65
Transfer income	1,888	1,942	0.97
of which, pensions	3,824	5,137	0.74
Sideline production income**	981	466	2.11
Income in kind	248	285	0.87

*N = 49 women, 59 men
**N = 29 women, 30 men

TABLE 5.6. Average Number of Years of
Education of Those Older than 15, by Sex,
1995 (years)

Urban	
Men	10.7
Women	9.8
Rural	
Men	6.6
Women	4.9

TABLE 5.7. Frequency of Second Job, by Sex, 1988 and 1995

Rural		
Men	4,783 (30.8%)	609 (5.4%)
Women	3,483 (24.8%)	184 (1.9%)
Urban		
Men	147 (1.5%)	68 (1.1%)
Women	64 (0.7%)	42 (0.7%)

sale reallocation of labor brought about by the shift from collective organization to market orientation, and especially the move from farming to non-agricultural pursuits, second jobs were a temporary transitional element that faded away as the shift was completed. The vast majority (84%) of respondents with second jobs in 1988 were farmers in their primary occupation. At that time, 92% of the rural employed in our sample were primarily farmers. By 1995, this share had dropped to 82%.

As Table 5.5 shows, the transition to a market economy has created some new opportunities for women, notably the development of an informal sector where private enterprises can flourish, as well as the mushrooming of TVEs and various ownership types categorized in Chinese statistics as "other," and comprising partnerships, jointly owned businesses, shareholding corporations, and foreign-invested enterprises. In 1995, women comprised almost half of all workers in the "other" sector (UNDP, 1999a). However, transition has also brought new pressures on women in the labor force. Old sexist prejudices have resurfaced in many forms, including job advertisements specifying "men only" or requiring that female applicants be young and attractive. There have been many complaints that women are the last to be hired and the first to be fired. National figures show them to be over-represented among the unemployed and among those laid off from ailing state enterprises (UNDP, 1999a).[15] Our data are consistent with this conclusion (Table 5.8): we find that women were a preponderant majority of those unemployed throughout 1995 and a smaller majority of those unemployed for part of the year. Among the latter, women's duration of unemployment averaged about one-third of the year, some 25 days longer than men's.

Although women face problems in both city and countryside, the urban-rural gap evidently plays a major role with respect to this issue as well. The worst problems faced by girls and women—domestic violence, kidnapping and sale of women, deprivation of education, the

TABLE 5.8. Shares of Women and Men among Employed and Unemployed, and Average Duration of Unemployment, Urban China, 1995

	Women	Men
Employed all year (percent of total)	47	53
Unemployed part of year (percent of total)	53	47
Unemployed throughout year (percent of total)	63	37

Note: For those unemployed part of the year, average duration of unemployment was 127 days for women and 102 days for men.

feminization of agriculture, and differentially poor care of female infants — are predominantly rural. Most rural-urban migrants are men, as we have seen; as migration enables men to make larger relative contributions to family income, their traditional social and political dominance is likely also to be strengthened. Thus, a good case can be made that a reduction in the urban bias characterizing Chinese social policy would — as an anticipated consequence — advance the position and status of women as well.

4. Problems in the Distribution of Health Care

Since the beginning of the transition period in the late 1970s, the health status of the Chinese people has continued to improve in general and on average. Life expectancy at birth rose to 70.8 years, according to official data; the infant mortality rate fell from 39 per thousand in 1980 to 31.4 in 1995, although some international observers, such as UNICEF, put the IMR somewhat higher, in the 40s per thousand (UNICEF, 1995). The immunization rate for children has reached about 85% and among much of the population, the incidence of infectious disease and of local endemic diseases (such as iodine deficiency disease) has been greatly reduced. Almost two-thirds of disease incidence in China now is caused by noncommunicable and chronic diseases and injuries, many traceable to lifestyle patterns (e.g., smoking) and environmental problems.

However, these accomplishments are distributed unevenly over the population, and there is some indication of increasing unevenness in recent years. Rural infant and under-five mortality rates are three times as high as urban rates. Under-five mortality in some poor rural counties approaches 10% of children (Hu 1997). World Bank analyses indicate that the national under-five mortality rate, regarded by UNICEF as the single best indicator of social development because it encompasses so many other indicators,[16] stopped declining in the early 1980s and stagnated until 1991, and that the percentage of rural children with very low height for age (a key indicator of malnutrition in children) increased from 1987 to 1992.[17]

One reason for the unevenness of health care is that public spending on health neglects the poor. In the words of the World Bank: "Government spending on health has not been effective in reaching China's poorest residents. . . . An analysis of public expenditure over eleven years shows that the allocation of public expenditure is skewed toward richer regions and, within regions, to the provinces growing fastest" (1997d).

More basic still, however, is the rapid shift in China's health care delivery system from a public health system oriented primarily toward disease prevention to a fee-for-service system emphasizing treatment. The Cooperative Medical System (CMS) covered more than 80% of the rural population and accounted for 20% of national health care spending at its peak in 1978. It rapidly disappeared with the collapse of the rural communes, reaching a low point of only about 2% coverage in 1987. Recently there have been attempts to resurrect it in some form, and in 1996 the government announced plans to increase its coverage of the rural population from the current level of about 10% to 80% by the year 2010.[18] In the meanwhile, although there are vestiges of the CMS still surviving in the villages, the social, risk-sharing funding mechanism that CMS supplied has largely disappeared and has been replaced mostly by private, out-of-pocket payment for medical services. One result is that the poorer rural residents, despite having a health and nutrition status well below the average for rural China, use medical services at lower rates. Indications are that their use is constrained by demand, not by lack of adequate supply of medical facilities (UNDP, 1999a), and the demand constraint is simply their inability to pay for increasingly costly medical care.

With the precipitous disappearance of the CMS, rural medical care now must be paid for by the patient. This suggests that income has become an important determinant of spending on medical care. To examine this hypothesis more closely, we look at the average per capita expenditure on medical care by income decile of the rural population, as shown in Figure 5.3.

Clearly, income and medical spending are related. The richest decile of the rural population spends 2.6 times as much on medical care as the poorest decile, and there is a fairly smooth upward progression

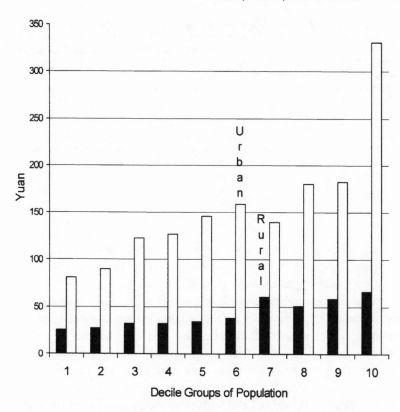

Figure 5.3. Medical Spending Per Capita, by Income Decile, 1995

in medical spending from the latter to the former. Yet the amounts involved are quite small relative to income, suggesting that health care is still widely affordable. Of the roughly 8,000 households in our rural sample, 7,049 reported having some medical expenses in 1995 (Table 5.9). Some 88% of these expenses were paid out of pocket, the average amount being 224 yuan per household, or only about 2% of average rural household income. The per capita out-of-pocket expense—55 yuan—was three times its level in 1988, a rate of increase about the same as that of nominal rural income. Yet the per capita medical expense in 1995 comes to under 5% of our standard poverty threshold (see Table 4.3), and to about 10% of the official poverty line for 1995. Perhaps it is because the cost of medical care is still so modest that household medical spending in our rural sample, despite the evidence of Table 5.10, is almost independent of household per capita

TABLE 5.9. Rural Medical Spending and its Sources, 1995

	No. of Households	Average Expenditure
Average total household expenditure		
on medical care in 1995	7,049	237
Out of pocket expenditure	6,195 (88%)	224
Paid by government or collective	152 (2%)	286
Paid by medical insurance	59 (1%)	334

Note: The components add up to 91% of total household medical expenditures. There is no category of "other" for this item. But possible other sources to account for the remainder include work units and relatives.

income. Thus, a simple regression yields a coefficient on income that is highly significant, but the regression explains less than 3% of the variation in per capita medical spending.[19]

A similar finding holds with respect to urban medical spending. The financing of medical care in the urban areas has also been coming increasingly from user fees. In the past, the vast majority of urban residents worked for state enterprises and had their health care provided by the government or their work unit. However, the increasing financial difficulties afflicting many state enterprises, and the public sector in general, have caused this system to erode rapidly. At the same time, with the growth of private and other non-state forms of ownership, the proportion of the urban population working in the state sector has diminished markedly. Although various insurance schemes

TABLE 5.10. Medical Spending Per Capita by Income Decile, 1995 (Yuan)

Decile	Rural	Urban
1	25	81
2	27	90
3	32	123
4	32	127
5	34	146
6	38	159
7	61	140
8	51	181
9	59	183
10	66	331

have appeared, there is as yet no national replacement for the failing system.

This situation is depicted in Table 5.11, which shows how urban Chinese working in various ownership sectors finance their medical care. Almost 80% of our sample worked in the state and local sector. Although the great majority of these still had their medical care provided by the government or work unit, a significant proportion paid for it through medical insurance or out of pocket. Half of those working in the urban collective sector (about 16% of the sample) and in Sino-foreign joint ventures (0.95%) continued to depend on work unit or government; the other half depended largely on self-finance. The fastest-growing sectors, private and individual workers, overwhelmingly self-financed their medical care.

The differentiation of the economy is thus leading to a parallel differentiation in means of financing medical care, leaving an increasing number of urban residents having to pay for it out of pocket. This is directly apparent in Table 5.12, which shows direct personal spending on medical treatment by ownership sector of work unit. As would be expected, those working in the state or local state sector paid the least—under 200 yuan—for medical care, while the self-employed or those working in individual enterprises paid almost 700 yuan.

Is the distribution of urban medical care becoming dependent on personal income, which, as we have seen, is distributed increasingly unequally? The third column of Table 5.10 shows a clear relation between income decile and per capita expenditure on medical care. The richest urban decile spends four times as much as the poorest, and the richest quintile three times as much as the poorest. Yet, as in the rural

TABLE 5.11. Type of Medical Coverage by Ownership Sector, Urban China, 1995

Ownership Sector of Work	Provided by State or Unit (%)	Medical Insurance	Entirely Self-Financed (%)	Other (%)
Local state	69.6	10	13.3	7.2
Urban collective	50	12.9	28	9
Private	5.7	5.7	84.9	3.8
Self-employed/individual enterprise	5.2	1	90.7	3.1
Sino-foreign joint venture	49	16.6	31.7	2.8

Note: Insufficient responses were received to give results for foreign-owned and TVE sectors. Rows may not add up exactly to 100% due to rounding errors.

TABLE 5.12. Medical Spending Per Capita, by Ownership Sector of Work, Urban China, 1995

Ownership Sector	No. of Observations	Yuan
Central or provincial state enterprise	2,402	194
Local state enterprise	4,973	199
Urban collective	1,469	232
Private enterprise	33	413
Self-employed/individual enterprise	95	680
Sino-foreign joint venture	85	523
Other	50	366
Sum of N for categories	9,123	

Note: Insufficient responses were received to report results for foreign-owned and TVE sectors.

case, spending levels were still modest relative to income. The average medical expense for urban sample residents who had such expenses in 1995 was 174 yuan. Although this was 8.5 times the level of spending in 1988—a rate of increase more than twice that of nominal urban income per capita—it still came to only about 3% of urban per capita disposable income. Perhaps because urban like rural medical costs remain low, we find that in the cities, as in the countryside, income has virtually no effect on medical expenditures. That is, a regression of medical spending on urban per capita income and a dummy representing sector of employment yields coefficients that, while highly significant, together explain a negligibly small proportion of the total variation in medical spending.[20]

Thus, within both the rural and urban populations, increased income differentiation and the commercialization of medical care had not, by 1995, resulted in significant differentiation in household spending on medical care. These findings might not hold for the poorest inhabitants of both city and countryside, who are probably underrepresented in our samples. Nevertheless, between urban and rural populations there was a large gap in both average income (2.4 to 1, by our estimate) and average spending on medical care (3.2 to 1). Moreover, the most dramatic differences in health status also follow the urban–rural divide: rural infant and under-five mortality rates average three times their urban counterparts, and rural maternal mortality rates are 2.2 times the urban ones. Thus, as it does for other aspects of human development in China, the urban–rural divide looms large as the most basic cause of inequitable distribution of health care. This suggests that, as China replaces the eroding system of work unit-based health care delivery in the public sector, it should vigorously pursue its announced plan of reestablishing a risk-sharing cooperative medical system for financing rural health care, and it should seek to bring to the rural majority health resources closer in quantity and quality to those enjoyed by the urban population.

Moreover, the relation between income and medical spending, even if still insignificant on the whole as a determinant of medical spending, is worrisome in the context of rapidly increasing income inequality, especially with medical costs increasing faster than real incomes. China's plan to rebuild a system of cooperative medical care in the countryside and a social insurance system to replace the failing enterprise-based one in the cities takes on added urgency in this context.

APPENDIX: Human Development Index by Province in 1995

Province	HDI Rank	GDP Rank	GDP Rank Minus HDI Rank	GDP Index	Human Development Index (HDI)	Change in HDI Value, 1990 to 1995
Shanghai	1	1	0	0.969	0.885	2.2
Beijing	2	2	0	0.960	0.876	13.3
Tianjin	3	3	0	0.954	0.859	6.1
Guangdong	4	4	0	0.850	0.814	16.2
Zhejiang	5	5	0	0.814	0.785	15.8
Jiangsu	6	6	0	0.724	0.760	12.3
Liaoning	7	8	1	0.708	0.756	5.8
Fujian	8	7	-1	0.709	0.729	14.1
Shandong	9	9	0	0.604	0.704	7.9
Heilongjiang	10	10	0	0.526	0.676	5.3
Hainan	11	11	0	0.488	0.674	9.3
Hebei	12	12	0	0.464	0.670	7.2
Jilin	13	13	0	0.451	0.659	5.0
Shanxi	14	17	3	0.352	0.627	2.1
Xinjiang	15	14	−1	0.438	0.619	2.6
Henan	16	16	0	0.358	0.618	6.0
Hubei	17	15	−2	0.388	0.609	3.1
Guangxi	18	18	0	0.332	0.605	5.7
Anhui	19	19	0	0.328	0.600	6.6
Hunan	20	23	3	0.320	0.592	4.4
Sichuan	21	24	3	0.308	0.582	5.0
Inner Mongolia	22	25	3	0.296	0.578	0.7
Jiangxi	23	20	−3	0.327	0.577	4.8
Ningxia	24	22	−2	0.323	0.571	2.8
Shaanxi	25	27	2	0.259	0.570	2.0
Yunnan	26	26	0	0.289	0.526	3.1
Gansu	27	29	2	0.216	0.514	0.9
Qinghai	28	20	−8	0.326	0.503	0.5
Guizhou	29	30	1	0.172	0.494	2.4
Tibet	30	28	−2	0.226	0.391	0.3

Sources: The HDIs for China's provinces in 1990 and 1995 were calculated by Li Shi for the *China National Human Development Report 1997*. Li's sources are as follows: (1) Lu Lei, Hao Hongsheng and Gao Ling "Table of Provincial Life-expectancy in China in 1990", *Population Studies* (in Chinese), May 1994; (2) SSB, *China Regional Economy: A Profile of 17 Years of Reform and Opening-Up*, China Statistical Press, 1996; (3) *Data of National 1% Population Survey 1995*, China Statistical Press, 1997; (4) China Education Commission, *Statistical Yearbook of China Education 1995*, People's Education Press, 1996; (5) *China Population Yearbook 1996*.

Notes: (1) GDP per capita is in 1990 prices. (2) Provincial price indices used for adjustment of GDP per capita are those of retail prices. (3) Life expectancy index is based on figures of provincial life expectancy in 1990; since life expectancy changes very slowly, this should have little impact on the HDI estimates.

6

Explaining the Increase in Inequality and the Decline in Poverty Reduction

. . . .

1. Introduction

Between 1988 and 1995, real per capita GDP in China increased at an annual rate of 8.1% per year—which amounts to an aggregate growth of 72% when compounded over seven years—according to official estimates. Unfortunately, China's unprecedented growth during this period was accompanied by a sharp increase in the inequality of income distribution. The result, as we have shown, is an unimpressive record of poverty reduction. The head count index of broad rural poverty declined by less than one-fifth, probably by only one-eighth. Although extreme forms of overall rural poverty declined somewhat more, there was an increase in rural poverty in some parts of the heartland of central China, as well as in more remote and resource-poor regions. Overall urban poverty rose. Even among the rich coastal provinces there are examples of rising incidence of poverty.

In this chapter, we try to provide an analysis of the major factors responsible for China's poor performance on income distribution and poverty reduction during this period of rapid growth. Changes in growth, distribution, and poverty are interrelated. Given the rate of growth, there is a threshold rate of increase in inequality beyond which any faster rise is translated into an increase in poverty. Similarly, given the rise in inequality, there is a threshold rate of growth that is necessary to prevent poverty from increasing. In the analysis of this relationship, a frequently missed link is that between aggregate GDP and personal income. Distributional inequality and the poverty threshold

103

are both measured in terms of personal income; thus, the particular rate of growth that is relevant for analyzing the factors affecting inequality and poverty is that of personal income. If the GDP elasticity of personal income is low, the effect on poverty of a fairly high growth in GDP can be offset by that of a moderate rise in inequality, so that poverty increases. We begin this chapter by considering the GDP elasticity of personal income, move on to examine the causes of increased inequality, and conclude by discussing the factors responsible for the poverty outcome.

As noted in Chapter 1, a principal purpose of this study is to explore the link between the reorientation of China's development strategy since the middle of the 1980s and the break in the nation's performance in income distribution and poverty reduction. We shall therefore try to analyze the extent to which each specific factor behind the inequality and poverty outcome was influenced by China's rapid integration with the global economy during the period under review.

2. Gap Between Growth in GDP and Growth in Personal Income

If one uses the official GDP estimates, the GDP elasticity of personal income turns out to have been relatively low, at under 0.6 during the period under review. Per capita GDP increased at 8.1% per year, while the growth rate in personal income was much slower—at most, 4.71% per year for rural China and 4.48% per year for urban China.[1] Might the gap between the growth rate of GDP and that of personal income be due to an overestimation of the former in the official national accounts? The World Bank, for example, has argued that the growth rate in GDP might have been overestimated. According to its estimates, real per capita GDP grew at a rate that was about 1.3 percentage points below the officially estimated rate for the years 1986 to 1995. If the same holds true for the subperiod 1988–1995, then the alternative rate would be 6.8% rather than the official 8.1%. This is still substantially higher than our estimated growth of personal income, and it raises the GDP elasticity of personal income from less than 0.6 to less than 0.7, which is still quite low.[2] To understand the consequences of the increase in inequality for mass living standards, the increase in the Gini ratio must be juxtaposed against the more modest rates of growth of personal income, rather than against the much higher rates of growth of GDP.

In the period when poverty was rapidly diminishing, between 1978 and 1985, the growth in personal income was much faster. We do not have estimates of these growth rates according to our comprehensive definition, but per capita personal income according to the SSB definition increased at 13.1% per year in the villages and over 5% per year in the towns and cities.

The divergence between aggregate growth rate and the growth in personal income during the period 1988–1995 is due mainly to macroeconomic policies affecting the distribution of incremental GDP among households, government, and enterprises, and between consumption and accumulation. Prominent among the instruments that were used to bring this about were policies concerning subsidies, taxes, and the system of remuneration by the state and collective enterprises. In urban areas, net subsidies and transfers as a proportion of per capita income declined from 39% in 1988 to only 11% in 1995. The failure on the part of official data to take much of these subsidies into account leads to a serious overestimation of urban income growth. In rural China, there occurred both a decline in the growth rate of agricultural output and, for about six years after 1988, a decline in agriculture's terms of trade. In 1994 these terms of trade improved sharply, and they retained their gain in the two following years.[3] It is quite possible that the relatively favorable trend in the incidence of rural poverty between 1988 and 1995 was due substantially to the belated improvement in agriculture's terms of trade beginning in 1994.

The exact details of the mechanism driving the wedge between the rates of growth in GDP and personal income cannot be determined because of the lack of transparency of China's system of national accounts. It seems, however, to have been driven largely by the tendency of the political economic system to exert constant upward pressures on investment and savings. As discussed in earlier chapters, our survey suggests that very little of investment was directly carried out by households; when households directly undertake investment, they must do so as business entities that have not been captured by the survey. Since investment is carried out by non-household entities, a rise in the ratio of investment to GDP must call for a redistribution of resources away from households and in favor of non-household entities. This can, of course, be done by borrowing from households, and in China this appears to have taken place to a degree. But the large gap between growth in personal income and growth in GDP strongly suggests a redistribution of income from households to non-household entities. The inverse movement of the rate of growth of personal income and the rate of investment and saving lends strong support to this view, although the mechanism of this redistribution is not transparent.

"Investment hunger," especially by the local governments that have wielded increasing authority through the 1980s and 1990s and that have no responsibility for national macroeconomic stability, is not a new phenomenon in contemporary China. In pre-reform days as well, periods of economic decentralization were characterized by runaway investment by local governments operating in an environment of chronic shortage and without significant budget constraints.[4] The classic case was the "great leap forward" of 1958–1960, when the "accumulation rate" — roughly equal to purchases of fixed and working capital as a fraction of net domestic material product — reached the unprecedented level of 43% (see Riskin, 1987, Chap. 6).

In the late 1970s, however, the government identified overaccumulation as a serious imbalance needing correction. Early in the reform period, strong administrative pressure was exerted to reduce accumulation by lowering investment rates and shifting resources away from the producer goods sector and into consumer goods production. Agricultural reforms were put in place, agriculture's terms of trade were significantly improved, and farm incomes soared. The result of all this was a sharp rise in personal income and consumption and a fall in the rate of domestic saving (see Table 6.1).

The Sixth Five-Year Plan, covering the period 1981–1985, was modest, setting very low growth targets, calling for continued restraint in investment, and focusing on efforts to improve efficiency. However, actual economic growth (averaging about 10% annually) benefited from unanticipated productivity gains, especially from the new reforms in agriculture, and left the Plan far behind (see Naughton, 1995).

Efforts to restrain investment were soon relaxed. The domestic savings rate crept upward again from its 1981 low to regain the pre-reform level in 1985, and it continued to advance from there to reach a staggering 42% of GDP in 1995. This trend was associated with a reduced agricultural growth rate and stagnating farm incomes in the second half of the 1980s, and with a collapse of credit restraint on the part of the government, which permitted virtually uncontrolled bank financing of the expansive investment plans of local governments. The

TABLE 6.1. Domestic Saving Rates (Percent of GDP)

1978	34.1	1982	31.6	1987	38.0	1991	37.0
1979	31.7	1983	31.3	1988	37.5	1992	37.0
1980	30.0	1984	32.0	1989	36.5	1993	40.2
1981	27.9	1986	36.3	1990	37.3	1995	42.0

Source: World Bank (1995a, 1997f).

Note. These estimates of saving rates are based on official GDP estimates. The results of our survey suggest that GDP is significantly underestimated. An upward adjustment of GDP, based on the survey data, would lower the savings rate in 1995 to about 37.5%. This is still one of the highest rates ever attained by any country.

accelerating inflation that resulted led to a draconian administrative austerity program in 1988 and 1989, which produced a deep recession—one of the elements feeding into the 1989 events in Tiananmen Square. Savings rates temporarily abated in those two years, but they resumed an upward drift again to the peak in 1995.

The government during this period evidently chose to deal with the increasingly complex problems of the transition, such as the threat of rising unemployment from reforming state enterprises, by permitting the fastest possible growth consistent with maintaining a tolerable inflation level. With administrative decentralization depriving the central government of direct control over investment allocation, and with tax collection resting largely in the hands of local governments, the center could resort only to credit expansion to finance its own priority investments and was unwilling to pay the political price of restricting localities' use of credit. One result was a soaring investment rate and an ensuing wedge between growth of GDP and that of personal income.

China might have permitted a faster growth in personal income if it had financed a part of the acceleration in the rate of investment by an inflow of external capital, an opportunity that China's integration with the global economy provided. As discussed in Chapter 1, this option was rejected. Indeed, the vast inflow of FDI in the 1990s was not allowed to drive the domestic savings rate below the rate of investment; instead, there was a meteoric rise in the volume of international reserves. This, of course, appears to have been a prudent decision in light of the financial crisis that hit many East Asian economies in 1997. Be that as it may, the particular way that China chose to manage its integration with the global economy appears at least partly to explain the wedge between the growth rate in GDP and the growth rate in personal income.

3. Sources of Increased Inequality in Income Distribution

In this section we discuss the principal sources of increased inequality in China. Although we focus on the factors suggested by the findings of the survey, we also consider a few outstanding macroeconomic trends.

Distribution of Land and of Access to Wage Income in Rural China

Many of the reforms and institutional changes in China have been disequalizing at the level of the distribution of household income. The replacement of collective agriculture by peasant farming was by far the most important institutional change of the reform period. Its disequalizing effect, however, was limited by strict measures to ensure an equal per capita access to land within each village. Over the years, researchers and policymakers have wondered whether the egalitarianism of the initial distribution of land has held or given way to increasing polarization. Our surveys have provided a reasonably conclusive, if surprising, answer to this question.

Table 6.2 shows land distribution and its contribution to income inequality in China in 1988 and 1995. Between these two years, the distribution of land actually became more equal, as is shown by the decline in the estimated Gini ratio. The concentration ratio—which measures inequality of land distribution over *all income recipients*, rather than over landholders—can be thought of as a measure of the contribution of landholding to income distribution. Even in 1988, land distribution had a strongly egalitarian effect on rural income distribution: its concentration ratio was a tiny proportion of the Gini ratio of income distribution. By 1995, the concentration ratio for "unadjusted" land had dropped to zero—indicating that land was absolutely equally accessible to all income groups—while the concentration ratio for "adjusted" land had fallen further from the already low value in 1988 (see the note to Table 6.2 for definitions of adjusted and unadjusted land).[5] Contrary to the concern expressed by some, the evolution of land distribution in rural China since decollec-

TABLE 6.2. Distribution of Per Capita Landholdings

	1988	1995
Gini Ratio		
Unadjusted land	0.499	0.431
Adjusted land	0.465	0.414
"Concentration Ratio"		
Unadjusted land	0.021	0.001
Adjusted land	0.063	0.051

Note: "Unadjusted land" is total land area irrespective of the proportion irrigated, while "adjusted land" counts an irrigated hectare as equivalent of 2 hectares of unirrigated land. The Gini ratio is estimated from the Lorenz distribution of per capita land, in which individuals are ranked according to per capita landholding. The concentration ratio is estimated from the Lorenz distribution of per capita land, in which individuals are ranked according to per capita income. These estimates are from Brenner (2000).

tivization has been one of the few positive aspects of rural income distribution.[6] The equality of access to land has been the main reason that income from farming is the most equalizing component of rural income, as is shown by its low concentration ratio of 0.281. Moreover, it has stood in the way of the development of a class of landless laborers at the lower end of the income distribution, and it has constituted the most important de facto source of income security in the villages, given the absence of an organized social safety net for most of rural China. Nor has such equality been inconsistent with rapid agricultural growth, averaging over 6% per year from 1980 to the mid-1990s.[7]

Whereas farm income is highly equalizing, income from wages is a highly disequalizing component of rural income. Between 1988 and 1995, wages not only became more disequalizing (their concentration ratio rose from 0.710 to 0.738), but their share in rural income also increased sharply from 8.7% to 22.4%. Unequal access to wage income was the single most important source of increased rural inequality during the period under review. Unequal access to wage income, in turn, is due to unequal growth of off-farm employment opportunities in different regions. Richer provinces have a far greater preponderance of rural wage employment than poorer provinces (Table 6.3).

Once again, it is important to note how the changes discussed above were closely related to the redirection of China's development strategy. Reduced growth of farm income was a direct consequence of the shift of emphasis away from the rural economy and in favor of integration with the global economy. The latter was responsible for an accentuation of inequality between the rich coastal provinces and the rest of the country. This, as shown above, was a major factor behind the inequality of the distribution of rural wage employment.

TABLE 6.3. Percent of Rural Household Income
Derived from Wage Employment

Five Richest Provinces		Five Poorest Provinces	
Beijing	52	Gansu	16
Guangdong	25	Guizhou	11
Jiangsu	29	Shanxi	19
Zhejiang	31	Yunnan	10
Shandong	37	Hunan	10

Urban Wages and Employment

The structure of urban wages, long kept highly equal at the cost of fostering widespread disincentive to work, was gradually differentiated. The expansion of private and foreign enterprises allowed rewards for entrepreneurship and skill to be differentiated from rewards for ordinary labor. Reform in state and collective enterprises also gradually permitted a greater differentiation of wage structure. The concentration ratio of urban wages increased sharply, from 0.178 in 1988 to 0.247 in 1995; however, this must be considered a desirable change, leading to a more efficient structure of labor remuneration. Furthermore, wages in 1995 were still an equalizing source of urban income insofar as their concentration ratio was lower than the urban Gini ratio.

Chinese policymakers clearly hoped that labor-intensive industrialization would bring about a rapid expansion of employment, which would offset the growing inequality of wage distribution and prevent a rise in urban poverty. Economic theory suggests that increased integration with the global economy, leading to a restructuring of production in favor of goods that use abundant factors intensively, should facilitate this outcome. Unfortunately, industrialization in the period of globalization has so far been remarkably employment-hostile. Contrary to the theoretical expectation that freer trade should increase the employment intensity of growth, and despite considerable empirical evidence that export industries that have grown rapidly are indeed largely labor-intensive, the output elasticity of employment in China's industries fell drastically.

The output elasticity of employment for all industries was only 0.27 during the decade 1984–1994, far lower than it was in the past and than it is in contemporary East Asian developing countries.[8] But this figure encompasses all kinds of industries, including the fast-growing ones in rural China. The employment hostility of China's urban industrial growth during the period under review is even greater, as is illustrated by the output elasticities shown in Table 6.4.

The output elasticity of employment for urban industries as a whole has been dismally low. The most important component, state industry, has an elasticity not significantly different from zero, while that of collective industry is actually negative. Between them, these two ownership categories in 1995 accounted for 89% of all formal employment in the industrial sectors covered by Table 6.4 (SSB, 1996, p. 96). Only in industries under private and other new forms of ownership did output growth go hand in hand with employment growth.

A principal reason why the collective and state enterprises performed so poorly in terms of employment creation is that, with the

TABLE 6.4. Output Elasticity of Employment in Urban
Industries, 1988–1995

All industries	0.037
State enterprises	0.032
Collective enterprises	−0.176
Enterprises under private and other ownership	0.874

Note: Industrial sectors included are manufacturing, mining, power, water and gas. Elasticities are *b* coefficients in the fitted regression equation: Log Employment = *a* + *b* Log Output Index, for each category. Data have been obtained from SSB, 1989, 1990 and 1997. The estimated elasticity coefficients are significant at 1% level for collective enterprises and enterprises under private and other ownership; 5% level for all industries; and no reasonable level of probability for state enterprises. In other words, the elasticity for state enterprises is not significantly different from zero at any reasonable level of probability. Note that for private and other forms of enterprises, employment data are comprehensive, but the output index refers to private industries only. Since the growth in output of private industries was broadly similar to the growth in output of industries under other forms of ownership, this should not have a large effect on the estimated elasticity.

growth of market orientation at home and greater integration into the world economy, they were subjected to increased competition from domestic and foreign private enterprises. China's state and collective enterprises responded to this competition by reducing the "concealed unemployment" they had inherited from the past as a consequence of the policy of guaranteed job security for all. The observed low output elasticity of employment is actually the net result of two divergent trends: (1) a high output elasticity of employment at constant intensity of employment per worker; and (2) a rise in the intensity of employment per worker resulting from a reduction in the number of redundant workers. Once the transition is completed and the concealed unemployment in state and collective enterprises eliminated, China's industries should become more efficient, and the observed output elasticity of employment should rise. However, there is also some disquieting evidence of the adoption of more capital-intensive technologies by enterprises. Thus, net value of fixed assets per worker in industry increased from 15,897 yuan in 1990 to 53,478 yuan in 1996; for state enterprises, the increase was from 18,530 to 51,755 yuan.[9] A rapid increase in capital intensity fits very poorly with China's basic situation of labor surplus and growing unemployment. With both factors at work, the process of transition has been characterized by very slow growth of employment,[10] and this has prevented the benefits of growth from being widely spread among the urban population, with consequent adverse effects on inequality and the incidence of poverty. Once again, this phenomenon is closely related to the process of integration with the global economy. Globalization accentuated the impetus on the part of state and collective enterprises to become lean, both in order to face the competitive pressure that openness to the global economy generated and to increase their attractiveness to FDI enterprises as possible collaborators.

China's urban labor force numbered about 198 million workers in 1996. Of these, 57% worked in state enterprises, 15% in urban collective enterprises, and 12% in private or individual enterprises.[11] The remainder were distributed over various other ownership forms, such as domestic and foreign-domestic joint ventures and foreign-owned enterprises (SSB, 1997). About 28 million state sector workers (including disguised unemployed and laid-off workers, discussed below) are estimated to be redundant. The low output elasticity of employment is largely a story of the increasing rate of disgorgement of workers from state and collective enterprises. With growing de facto unemployment has come growing urban poverty.

The Ministry of Labor put the rate of *registered* unemployment in 1996 at 3% of the urban labor force (*China Daily*, 11 March 1997). By October 1997, registered unemployment had risen to 8 million, up from 6 million in 1996 and 3.5 million in 1991. Although the upward trend through the 1990s has been clear even from the figures for registered unemployment, the absolute numbers greatly understate actual unemployment because they include only those registered with local labor bureaus. The unemployed who have not registered are omitted, as are the large number of workers who have been laid off by troubled state enterprises with which they retain a formal connection. A recent estimate put actual unemployment in late 1998 at around 16 million, for an unemployment rate between 7.9 and 8.5 percent, including unregistered unemployed, laid-off workers, and unemployed rural–urban migrants.[12] One source has cited a State Statistical Bureau estimate that as many as 87% of the urban poor are state sector workers and retirees and their families (*China Daily*, 16 August 1997).

Thus, official statistics indicate a strong correlation between urban poverty and unemployment. We approach this topic by asking two questions: What proportion of the urban poor, by our definitions, are unemployed? And what proportion of the unemployed are poor? We also examine the labor force participation rates of the poor.

To begin, we calculate crude labor force estimates by adding together those respondents who report being employed and those who report being unemployed. Those reporting their status as unemployed came to 3.3% of the labor force, so estimated, which closely approximates official figures for registered unemployment. However, we suppose that respondents followed the official definition of unemployment, which, as discussed above, excludes workers laid off from jobs in state enterprises. Unfortunately, "laid off" was not a category in our question on employment status. It is likely that some laid-off workers chose the category "other." If all people choosing "other" were in fact unemployed, the rate of unemployment would be 5.66%. Thus, we conclude that the true unemployment rate in our urban sample is between 3.3 and 5.7%.

In our probe for employment situation in 1995 as a whole, however, "unemployed" was specifically defined to include "laid off." About 8.5% of respondents reported being unemployed for all or part of 1995. Of these, 7.2% said they were unemployed for part of the year (the average number of days unemployed being 108), and 1.3% reported being unemployed during the entire year. Table 6.5 examines the rates of those reporting unemployment for all or part of 1995 among our three categories of poor, and also the labor force participation rates among the poor.

It is immediately clear that the urban poor suffer from two disadvantages that probably contribute significantly to their poverty. First, their labor force participation rates are from 21% to 24% below the average for the sample as a whole. Having fewer working members per household is a very substantial depressant of household per capita income, especially in a society in which there are very few major sources of income other than labor. Larger fractions of the poor were children of school or preschool age, full-time homemakers, and "other" (which we suspect captures some laid-off workers). A very slightly larger proportion were disabled. However, a substantially smaller fraction of the poor were retired.

TABLE 6.5. Unemployment Rates of the Urban Poor

Group of population	Labor Force Participation Rate (percent)	1995 Unemployed as Percent of Labor Force
Total urban sample	57.7	8.5
Broad poor	45.5	20.7
Deep poor	44.1	22.2
Extreme poor	45.7	25.3

Note: "Unemployed" here includes laid-off state enterprise workers and refers to those who were unemployed all or part of 1995.

Second, unemployment rates (in the sense we have defined them here) among the poor are from 2.4 to over 3 times as high as the average for the entire urban sample. The unemployment rate increased with the extent of poverty, being 20.7% for the broad poor and 25.3% for the extreme poor. Thus, it seems likely that unemployment was a major contributor to urban poverty.

Nonetheless, as Table 6.6 shows, the great majority of the unemployed were not poor. Even though poverty rates among the unemployed were roughly twice as high as among the urban population as a whole, about 85% of the unemployed had incomes above the broad poverty threshold. Evidently, most of the unemployed (including laid-off workers) had recourse to income from other family members, maintenance payments from their enterprises, informal jobs, or other sources.

Conversely, most of the labor force living in poverty were employed: 75% of the extreme poor, 78% of the deep poor, and 79% of the broad poor. Of course, as we have seen, the labor force participation rate itself was significantly smaller for the poor population than the non-poor. Nevertheless, working poor constituted almost half of the poor population and three-quarters or more of the poor labor force. State enterprises, in addition to laying off millions of workers, have stopped paying wages or have reduced wage payments to an estimated 10 million workers (as of spring 1998) who remained on the job (Hu Angang, 1998). This development probably contributed to the expansion of the population of working poor.

There is a sense in the Chinese discussions of this problem that the mushrooming growth of real unemployment is challenging the meager capacity of local governments and enterprises to provide maintenance and/or relief to those affected. Thus, the real income of laid-off workers is said to be dropping. In 1996, the average annual allowance was put at 925 yuan, well below our extreme poverty threshold (Hu Angang, 1998).

TABLE 6.6. Poverty Rates of the Urban Unemployed in 1995

Category of Poverty	Percent of Urban Population	Percent of the Unemployed
Non-poor	91.8	84.7
Broad poverty	8.2	15.3
Deep poverty	4.1	8.1
Extreme poverty	2.7	6.4

Public Finance and Access to Services

We have already shown that public finance — state taxes and subsidies, including those levied and paid by collectives — is highly regressive and a major source of inequality in both rural and urban China (see Chap. 3). Although the magnitude of urban subsidies has declined sharply in recent years, the estimates based on the survey show that the remaining net subsidies mainly benefit the higher income groups because of poor targeting. In recent years, changes in the volume and distribution of public and collective resources for education and health have resulted in a substantial reduction of poor people's access to these basic services (see Chap. 5 and Khan, 1996).

Continued Inequality Between Rural and Urban China

We noted in Chapter 3 that China's overall Gini ratio is greater than either the rural or urban Gini ratio because of the dominance of the disparity between rural and urban areas. Although the ratio between rural and urban per capita incomes did not rise significantly between 1988 and 1995 — indeed, it fell slightly at constant purchasing power — the proportion of total household income accruing to the richer of the two groups (i.e., the urban households) increased because of greater urbanization. This had a disequalizing effect on the overall income distribution for China.

Public policy in China has contributed to the persistence of high rural/urban inequality. For years after the mid-1980s, agriculture's terms of trade declined or stagnated. Only very recently has this changed somewhat. Public finance is strongly biased against rural society, which receives a disproportionately low share of public expenditure and investment. As shown in Chapter 2, rural households are subjected to a net tax while urban households receive a significant net subsidy. Once again, the bias against the rural sector, prevalent in both 1988 and 1995, represents a shift away from the agriculture-led growth prior to the mid-1980s toward a strategy thereafter that emphasized integration with the global economy.

Migration

One more factor contributing to China's increasing inequality has to do with the "floating population" of migrants. These people are not legal urban residents, whose number is rigidly controlled by a system of residence permits (although some migrants have obtained temporary permits). Although their presence in urban areas has been more or less tolerated, they have been excluded from the benefits received by full-status urban residents, such as access to (subsidized) public housing, social services, and public schooling for their children. The number of floating migrants in 1995 has been variously estimated—at about 72 million by a Labor Ministry survey, and at 84 million by the public security authorities—and thus amounted to between one-fifth and one-quarter of the officially registered urban population.[13] They are excluded from the estimates of urban poverty, as we have already pointed out; had they been included, urban poverty rates would have been higher and their rates of increase faster between 1988 and 1995.

Although it is well known that the poorest people are usually unable to reap the benefits of population mobility, the process of rural–urban migration has nevertheless probably had some dampening effect on both the incidence of rural poverty and the size of the urban/rural income gap, because such migration helps to reduce rural unemployment and underemployment, and it also provides income remittances to home villages from higher-paying urban jobs (see Li Shi, 2000). Thus, tolerance of the presence of migrants in the cities has helped to prevent a further worsening of China's income distribution and to alleviate overall poverty. This beneficial effect would be further strengthened were official discrimination against migrants ended and the incidence of poverty among migrants themselves reduced. Such a policy might, of course, encourage a greater flow of migration out of rural China, but that too would help to reduce overall inequality and poverty—if not urban inequality and poverty—by reducing the urban/rural income inequality from its extraordinarily high level.

Regional Inequality

Another major cause of the increase in inequality is the increased regional inequality that has been a concomitant of the strategy of greater integration with the global economy. China's eleven coastal provinces, with 40% of the country's population, account for 80% of its exports. Of these eleven provinces and Beijing, eight are ranked as the richest eight provinces in China; the other four of them are well above average in terms of per capita income. According to official estimates, these twelve provinces grew at an average rate that was 78% faster than the rate at which central and western provinces grew during the 1990s. This was due largely to the export-led development strategy of which the inflow of direct foreign investment, primarily located in the urban areas of these twelve provinces, was an integral part. To facilitate the success of the strategy, public resources and incentives were sharply tilted in favor of these richest and fastest-growing provinces. Most of China's poor live outside these provinces.[14]

The above factors go a long way toward explaining increased inequality; however, policymakers in China need to deepen their understanding of the phenomenon by analyzing the reasons why the rate of change in inequality varied so much among provinces, if indeed our estimates of changes in intraprovincial inequality are reasonably reliable despite the small size of the provincial samples. Why did the Gini ratio fall in rural Henan, Jilin, Hebei, and Beijing while it increased in the rest of rural China? Why was the rise in the Gini ratio in urban Anhui so much lower than the rise in the urban Gini ratio elsewhere in China? Unfortunately, the information processed from the survey itself does not illuminate these issues. Explanations for these phenomena are not suggested by differences in the composition of sources of income among provinces or some other similar information processed from the survey. One needs to go beyond the survey data to find answers to these important questions.

4. Growth, Inequality, and Poverty

The change in the incidence of poverty is determined by the growth in per capita personal income and the change in the distribution of personal income. The large lag of the growth in personal income behind the growth in GDP explains a part of the unsatisfactory performance in poverty reduction. Had a larger part of the growth in GDP been passed on to the households in the form of a rise in personal income, China's performance in poverty reduction would have been better.

Nevertheless, the growth in personal income that actually took place was very substantial by any standard. Had the distribution of personal income in rural and urban China in 1995 remained exactly the same as in 1988, the Head Count index of rural poverty would have declined by half, and the Head Count index of urban poverty would have been virtually eliminated. Thus, a very large responsibility for China's poor performance in alleviating poverty must be borne by the increase in inequality. The latter should, in this case, be measured by the relevant change in Lorenz distribution affecting the poor, rather than by the change in summary inequality measures (e.g., the Gini ratio).[15] But it is reasonable to hope that changes in Gini ratios would, by and large, capture the effect of redistribution on the poor so that a rise (fall) in the Gini ratio, other things remaining unchanged, would lead to an increase (fall) in the incidence of poverty. Tables 6.7 and 6.8 show growth rates in per capita incomes and changes in Gini ratios for rural and urban China and their provinces, along with changes in head count poverty, between 1988 and 1995.

For rural China as a whole, the rate of growth in per capita income was quite high (though much less than the rate of growth of per capita GDP), and the rate of increase in inequality was moderate. The result was a modest reduction in the incidence of poverty, though by much less than it would have been in the absence of a change in income distribution.

For urban China as a whole, income increased less rapidly than among the rural population, while the increase in inequality was far greater. The result was a rise in poverty (not in the most favorable of the indicators shown in Table 6.8, but in the indicators of extreme poverty and the indices, based on a more realistic CPI, shown in Chapter 4).

TABLE 6.7. Poverty, Growth, and Inequality in Rural China (Change Between 1988 and 1995)

	Percent Change in Head Count Poverty Index	Annual Growth in Per Capita Income	Percent Change in Gini Ratio
All China	−18.6	4.71	23.1
Gansu	−1.0	1.25	36.5
Shaanxi	−3.2	3.65	37.7
Guizhou	6.0	0.72	3.1
Henan	−61.7	6.45	−8.0
Shanxi	−4.6	0.85	1.3
Yunnan	−3.6	1.26	4.2
Anhui	−44.4	3.79	9.2
Jilin	−55.9	7.26	−4.5
Sichuan	32.6	0.62	28.3
Jiangxi	5.1	1.68	24.8
Shandong	−31.8	7.89	51.6
Hubei	23.2	1.98	34.6
Hebei	−24.1	2.54	−0.4
Liaoning	−18.9	2.02	2.1
Hunan	186.3	−3.30	18.4
Jiangsu	−83.1	11.66	2.1
Guangdong	8.3	7.11	27.5
Beijing	−85.1	9.33	−1.0
Zhejiang	−31.0	4.86	26.2

Note: Change in the Head Count index of poverty refers to the estimates of broad poverty without any adjustment in the CPI. Income changes are estimated by deflating 1995 per capita income by the unadjusted CPIs and comparing them with 1988 estimates.

TABLE 6.8. Poverty, Growth, and Inequality in Urban China (Change Between 1988 and 1995)

	Per Cent Change in Head Count Poverty Index	Annual Growth in Per Capita Income	Percent Change in Gini Ratio
All China	−2.4	4.48	42.5
Shanxi	−14.1	2.51	23.7
Henan	32.5	2.37	46.4
Anhui	−50.0	3.41	14.9
Hubei	43.2	3.34	42.9
Yunnan	−22.8	2.81	18.6
Liaoning	216.7	4.94	106.2
Jiangsu	−30.8	5.53	45.7
Gansu	104.8	3.94	124.2
Beijing	Increase	7.84	41.9
Guangdong	50.0	6.86	26.9

Note: Changes in head count poverty are based on estimates of broad poverty without any adjustment for CPI. Any of the other alternative measurements would make the changes more unfavorable and would show a rise in poverty for urban China as a whole. For Beijing, the rate of change cannot be calculated because the Head Count index for 1988 was zero. For methods of estimating growth rates in income, see note to Table 6.7.

Changes in broad poverty in individual rural provinces are much better explained by income growth than by changes in the Gini ratio (Table 6.7). Variation in income growth explains 60% of the variation in the Head Count index of broad poverty among provinces. Adding the change in Gini ratio as an additional explanatory variable increases the proportion of explained variation in changes in poverty to 63%.[16]

Even though high growth seems to be the decisive factor in achieving a reduction in poverty in rural China, the rise in the Gini ratio was modest in all the five provinces with rapidly declining broad poverty (negative in the case of Jilin). The province with the most rapid increase in broad poverty, Hunan, had not only a large fall in per capita income but also a moderately high increase in the Gini ratio. The other provinces with relatively high rates of increase in broad poverty—Sichuan and Hubei—experienced moderately large increases in inequality in addition to low growth.

Variation in the rate of change in broad poverty among urban areas of China's provinces is explained much better by the change in the Gini ratio than by the growth rate of income (Table 6.8). Change in the Gini ratio explains 63% of the variation in the rate of poverty reduction among urban provinces. Adding growth of income as an additional explanatory variable does not add to the explained variation at all.[17]

Liaoning is an example of a province with an explosive increase in poverty despite a higher than average growth in per capita income; the explanation lies in the more than doubling of the Gini ratio. Despite very high growth, poverty increased in Beijing and Guangdong as a result of moderately large increases in inequality. Anhui achieved a substantial reduction in poverty despite a significantly lower than average rate of growth in income because its increase in inequality was very modest—indeed, the lowest among the provinces.

5. Conclusion

China's poor performance in income distribution and poverty reduction, in the period of rapid growth that we call "the era of globalization," has been due to many causes, of which the most important have been discussed above. One of the notable features of these causes is that they are not as overtly dominated by deep-rooted structural and institutional factors—e.g., an unequal distribution of land and productive assets—as are the causes of inequality and poverty in most developing nations. Indeed, the equality of the distribution of land in China has prevented inequality and poverty from getting worse. Much of the cause of increased inequality and reduced poverty alleviation has resided in public policies related to such issues as macroeconomic management, fiscal system, enterprise reform, regional balance, and migration. Many of these policies were directly linked to the reorientation of China's development strategy from a preoccupation with the rural sector to integration with the global economy. Although such integration was essential for China's growth and efficiency, it was not accompanied by appropriate countervailing policies and actions to protect Chinese society from the disequalizing effects that the process of integration unleashed. As a result, there was increased regional concentration of the benefits of globalization, a dismally low output elasticity of employment in industries, and a widening of the urban/rural income disparity.

7

Policies for the Reduction of Inequality and Poverty

. . . .

1. Introduction

The analysis of the preceding chapters suggests the elements of a comprehensive strategy for arresting the trend toward increasing inequality and correcting the poor performance in poverty reduction. Chapter 6 helps to focus attention on the aspects of development policy that shape the pattern of income distribution. A comprehensive strategy for greater equality and less poverty must include *consistent* actions on a broad front, involving macroeconomic and institutional policies that determine the overall pattern of development, as well as microeconomic interventions to directly enhance the capabilities of poor households. Before outlining the elements of such a strategy, it will be useful to begin with a brief overview of China's official strategy on income distribution and poverty reduction.[1]

As we noted in the introductory chapter, China's reform program started with the presumption that, in the past, China had a distribution of income too equal to permit an efficient operation of the economy. An increase in inequality was therefore seen by the policymakers as a desirable outcome of the reform program. Since the beginning of reforms, China's income distribution has undergone a qualitative transformation from being one of the most equal among the developing Asian countries to being one of the more unequal; however, there has not been a systematic concern among policymakers about the distribution of income per se. In this sense, it cannot be claimed that China has a policy favoring greater equality in the distribution of income per

121

se. There has, however, been much discussion about one aspect of growing inequality: the increasing income gap between the relatively advanced coastal provinces and the more backward central and western ones. Political stability, which is the government's most important general goal, is seen to be potentially threatened by excessive regional polarization. Therefore, there have been efforts to encourage a greater flow of investment resources to the poorer western provinces.

There is also a great deal of official concern about the continued existence of absolute poverty. China's official poverty reduction strategy is regional in its structure and orientation and is based on the assumption that poverty is an exclusively rural phenomenon. It identifies 592 rural counties that are poor, on the basis of their per capita income,[2] and focuses on improving the average living standard in these counties through a package of micro-interventions, rather than on targeted interventions to improve the condition of the poor households themselves.

In January 1994, the State Council put into effect the National 8-7 Plan for Poverty Reduction, with the objective of lifting the officially estimated 80 million rural poor out of poverty in the remaining seven years of the second millennium.[3] The plan set the goal of bringing the average income of these counties — and of the overwhelming majority of the households therein — to 500 yuan or more at 1990 prices.[4] In addition, the plan set poverty alleviation goals for infrastructure development, education, vocational and technical training, sanitation, and family planning.

The state provides funds for poverty reduction activities through three main channels: the Ministry of Finance, the State Planning Commission, and the Agricultural Development Bank (ADB), a policy bank recently split off from the Agricultural Bank of China (ABC). Poverty reduction funds from the central government or ADB are available for use only in the designated 592 poor counties. The largest part of the funds consists of low-interest loans from the ADB for a variety of production activities. The planning commission funds are used for Food for Work projects for the construction of infrastructure and drinking water projects, often using local labor. Appropriations through the Finance Ministry are directed mainly to training activities.

Simultaneously, all government departments are called on to allocate a part of their own budget to help the development of the designated counties. In addition, international agencies, such as the United Nations Development Programme (UNDP) and the World Bank, as well as both domestic and international NGOs, have started operating in the poor counties. Recently, the Institute of Rural Development of the Chinese Academy of Social Sciences has pioneered a micro-credit program (modeled on that of Bangladesh's Grameen Bank) which has been implemented as a pilot program in some poor counties in Hebei.

It is impossible to judge to what extent the targeted program of improving the productivity of the poor areas has benefited the poor. The focus is on the development of the average income and productivity of these counties, even though some of the programs are ostensibly more specifically targeted to the poor households. Systematic evaluation of the impact of these programs on the poor is not available. Official sources claim that the number of rural poor has declined at an annual rate of 5 million as a result of the implementation of the program during the first two years. There is no way to judge the validity of this claim or to separate the effects of the 8-7 Plan from those of other economic trends.

There are three main inadequacies of the official Chinese strategy for poverty reduction.[5] First, quite apart from the question of whether these programs adequately look after the needs of the poor in the designated counties, there are two other large groups of poor that have been left out of the official poverty alleviation program. The SSB estimates that one-third of the rural poor live outside the officially designated poor counties, while some outside studies suggest that this ratio is as high as half.[6] The other group that has been omitted from the scope of the program is the urban poor—a group that, according to our estimates, has been growing rapidly.

Second, the structure, organization, and funding of the poverty reduction program do not permit a comprehensive approach that takes into account all of the needs of the poor, including health, nutrition, and education. This is due in part to lack of sufficient recognition of the need for such programs on the part of the leading authorities in charge of the poverty reduction program, and in part to their lack of both budget and authority to fashion and implement them.

The third major inadequacy of the program is the lack of complementarity between overall development policies and the micro-interventions under the 8-7 Plan. As our analysis in the preceding section shows, many development policies may actually have produced an outcome that was contrary to the objectives of the micro-interventions. Fostering economic growth through policies that steer resources away from poor areas and people, and then trying to compensate with a poverty alleviation program, turns out to have been an ineffective overall strategy for coping with poverty. Here as in other problem areas (education, the environment, unemployment, for instance), the tendency has been to substitute economic growth for effective social policy rather than to take advantage of the income dividends provided by rapid growth to fashion true solutions. In the slower growth environment that has already begun in China, the opportunities afforded by rapid growth will be much smaller, while the need for effective social policy will be much clearer.

2. Need for a Comprehensive Strategy

The experience of the past decade clearly shows that a high rate of growth by itself does not lead to the desired reduction of poverty. It is extremely important to reverse the forces of inequality which in the recent past prevented much of the potential reduction of poverty that growth could have provided. Furthermore, the problem cannot be dealt with by means of a plan that is independent of the overall development strategy. Components of development policy—for example, policies concerning regional balance in growth, macroeconomic policies for capital accumulation, or sectoral terms of trade and public finance—can affect household welfare far more powerfully than the kind of microeconomic interventions promoted by the 8-7 Plan, for the simple reason that the amount of resources shifted by such policies dwarfs the amounts available for the specific anti-poverty effort. It is therefore essential to ensure that the major components of development policy are consistent with the target of reducing poverty. China's strategy in this regard must also break the artificial barrier of the designated rural counties and target the poor in other rural locations and in the towns and cities. In the remainder of this chapter, we highlight the major changes in development policy and the urgent targeted interventions that should constitute the core of a comprehensive strategy for the reduction of poverty and inequality in China.

In the preceding chapter, we showed that many of the factors that have been responsible for the unfavorable distributional outcome were related to ongoing integration with the global economy. This calls for adjustments in the process of integration, not for abandoning it, which would greatly damage China's prospects for economic growth and efficiency. What is needed is a carefully formulated set of policies and actions to offset the adverse distributional consequences of integration with the world economy. Examples of such policies and actions are a shift of resources in favor of the rural economy, a better regional balance in development, and compensatory policies for the protection of laid-off workers, encompassing a restructuring of urban subsidies.

3. Reduction of Urban/Rural Gap and Policies for the Rural Economy

Even though the Gini ratio increased at a slower rate in rural than in urban China between 1988 and 1995, the degree of inequality continues to be higher for the rural than for the urban population. This is in contrast to the situation in most developing countries, where urban inequality is greater than rural. Although the poverty trend during 1988–1995 was more favorable in rural than in urban areas, poverty still is an overwhelmingly rural phenomenon. Well over 90% of the poor would be found in rural areas under any reasonable uniform urban and rural poverty threshold. China cannot win its war against poverty without a decisive strategy for the reduction of rural poverty.

In this context, the first target for action is the unusually large difference between average urban and rural incomes. The ratio of urban to rural per capita income was 2.42 in 1988 and 2.47 in 1995,[7] as compared with a ratio well below 2 in most developing Asian countries and often as low as 1.5.[8] As noted in section 1, China's commendable success in reducing poverty in the early years of reform was associated with a large reduction in the urban/rural income gap. Starting in 1984, however, this gap rose sharply and steadily until 1994. This period of rising urban/rural income gap witnessed a sharp reduction, and possibly an ultimate halt, in the rate of poverty reduction in rural China. We have also noted that the relatively favorable change in rural poverty between 1988 and 1995 may be due largely to developments at the very end of that period: 1995 was the first year in more than a decade in which the urban/rural income gap declined according to official estimates—a change that probably occurred principally because of an improvement in agriculture's terms of trade in 1994.

China's substantial urban/rural inequality was due in large part to policies discriminatory against the rural sector. Official farm procurement prices were quite low, resulting in adverse terms of trade for agriculture. Strict control of migration from rural to urban areas, on the other hand, deprived the rural population of the relief that migration affords in many developing societies in the form of income remittances and reduced demographic pressure. The more recent changes in policy toward population mobility and the need for further liberalization are discussed in section 7 below.

The growth of farm output also slowed since the mid-1980s. The decline in agricultural growth is partly explained by the failure of the terms of trade to continue to improve. In addition, it appears that too few resources were put into investment in agriculture. Government spending on agriculture, as a proportion of total government expenditure, fell from 13.6% in 1978 to 8.3% in 1985, and it stayed there until the mid-1990s (SSB, 1995, 1997).

One notes with some concern that official policy in China often appears to aim merely at reducing the *rate of increase* in the urban/rural disparity, rather than reducing the disparity itself. Thus, Prime Minister Li Peng's report on the Ninth Five-Year Plan, delivered at the National People's Congress on 5 March 1996, states: "During the Ninth Five-Year Plan period, the urban residents' per capita income spent on living expenses after allowing for price rises is expected to increase by about 5% annually and the per capita net income of the peasants is expected to increase by about 4% annually."

China should put a decisive end to its vacillation toward the rural sector by adopting a package of policies in which the following should be the major elements: (1) allow the terms of trade of the sector to be determined by economic forces without depressive public intervention; (2) improve the rural sector's share of public resources, including resources for health care and education; (3) promote rural non-farm activities; and (4) further liberalize control of population movement so as to permit a freer flow of people in search of economic and social opportunity.

Terms of Trade for Agriculture

As noted above, in recent years public policy has sought to improve agriculture's terms of trade in order to stimulate farm production and prevent widening of inequality between the urban and rural sectors. In 1994, farm purchase prices were adjusted sharply upward, causing grain prices to approach international levels and resulting in a significant improvement in agriculture's terms of trade. It is, however, essential that economic forces rather than artificial public intervention be allowed to determine the terms of trade. By now, a large majority of farm prices are determined by market forces, but grain prices are still subject to substantial government controls. The ending of such controls would further improve relative farm prices and have the added benefit of raising income in poorer central and western provinces that have a comparative advantage in grain production.[9]

Resources for Agriculture

Growth of farm output has also increased in very recent years in response to higher prices gained by the farmers. There is, however, no evidence that public resources for agriculture have grown, at least relative to GDP. Government expenditure on agriculture, as a proportion of total government expenditure, has continued at the low level to which it fell in 1985. Nevertheless, several of the constraints on growth of farm output are of the sort whose solution requires that government take a major role. The most important long-run constraint is the shortage of fresh water supplies, especially in Northern China. Conservation efforts, pricing changes, stepped-up treatment of municipal wastewater, large-scale projects to move water from the south (where it is abundant), and stringent efforts to reverse the poisoning of existing water supplies by the profligate use of farm chemicals are all necessary parts of a public program to address China's most threatening resource shortage. In addition, greater public support is needed for agricultural research, which the World Bank identifies as the biggest single factor in explaining China's agricultural growth. In the long run, government must also encourage the popularization of more environment-friendly and sustainable approaches to agriculture.[10] The recovery of agricultural growth may not be sustained unless there is an increase in agriculture's share of investment and other resources.

Access to Land

As analyzed in the preceding chapter, equality of access to land, the single most important productive resource for the rural majority of the population, has had a powerful effect in preserving and promoting equality of rural income distribution. So far, equality of access to land has been maintained. There has been a vigorous debate in China over the advisability of clarifying property rights in agriculture. Currently, there is considerable ambiguity about the length of time farmers may lease their land from the local government. Formal rules about this are often ignored and land redivided among a village's households when demographic changes occur. This casual approach to property rights is thought to harm incentives to improve the land. Nonetheless, the existing system has proved compatible with enormous increases in farm output while limiting the growth of rural inequality and preventing the emergence of a class of landless laborers that elsewhere in Asia constitutes the core of the rural poor. Moreover, there is evidence that the existing system is popular and thought reasonable by Chinese farmers.[11] It is essential that any changes in the land tenure system preserve these crucial advantages of the current system.

Non-Farm Rural Activities

We established in the preceding chapters that access to non-farm economic activities and wage employment are powerful factors enabling rural households to escape poverty. This issue has assumed increased urgency in view of the fact that employment in farming peaked in absolute terms in 1991 and started to decline thereafter. Little information is available about trends in non-farm rural employment outside the township and village enterprises (TVEs). Employment in TVEs grew rapidly and steadily during the 1980s at an average annual rate of 12%. In 1993, there was a net decline in TVE employment of 2.7%. Thereafter, employment growth in TVEs recovered, but only to half the rate of growth that was achieved in the 1980s (SSB, 1989, 1995, 1997).

Support for rural non-farm activities, including TVEs and small private enterprise, should be strengthened within the limits of the actual and/or potential comparative advantage of rural China for these activities. Access to credit, technical knowledge, and marketing facilities are some of the important forms that such support should take. Investment in infrastructure in poor areas is a precondition for the creation of healthy linkages between the rapidly growing modern industries in the coastal provinces and "infant" subcontracting in the rural areas of the poor provinces. Greater investment in education is necessary so that residents of poor rural areas will be able to take advantage of such linkages where they exist.

Part of the recent slowdown in TVE growth has been due to widespread market saturation. This is in turn a function in part of increasing inequality of distribution, and especially of the limited growth of rural incomes, since ownership rates of popular goods of all kinds are far lower in the countryside than in the city.[12] Greater equality would help to provide greater mass market demand and thus to stimulate China's limping TVE sector.

4. Regional Balance in Development

Increasing disparities among regions have been an important source of increasing inequality in China. Slow growth of the poorer areas has been a hindrance to China's capacity to reduce poverty. Regional disparities in China have mainly taken the form of a discrepancy between the rapidly growing provinces of the eastern (coastal) region and the slow-growing central and western regions.[13] This was not entirely the result of the higher profitability of investment in the eastern region; a good part of it has been due to policies that were discriminatory toward the poor regions. In the absence of comprehensive research on this subject, we can only give illustrations. For example, special privileges (concerning such matters as tax rates and profit repatriation rules) designed to attract foreign direct investment were long limited to already advantaged coastal regions, and so the benefits of globalization were concentrated in these regions. Poor and backward regions were prevented from competing for investment resources not only by their natural disadvantages but also by artificial administrative strictures. Similarly, the artificial depression of producer prices for grain has been detrimental to the growth of the rural areas of the central and western regions, which have a comparative advantage in grain production. Another example is the pricing of natural resources: vast quantities of coal, whose extraction uses up scarce supplies of fresh water, are taken out of poor areas of Shanxi Province at ex-factory prices that are extremely low and do not reach the poor villages at all. Shanxi's role as a supplier of coal to China and the world market appears to engender a net loss to the poor rural regions from which the coal comes.[14] These discriminatory policies need to be comprehensively catalogued and systematically ended.

There are signs that Chinese policymakers have become aware of the severity of the problem of regional polarization. In autumn of 1995, the Plenary Session of the Party Central Committee decided to shift the focus of the incentive system and of public expenditure to attract foreign direct investment to the central and western provinces. Development of the Western regions was a major theme of the Ninth National Peoples Congress meeting in March 2000.

5. Reversing the Disequalizing Effect of the Fiscal System and Transfer Payments

There are two aspects of the problem of the fiscal system with which we are concerned here. The first is the extreme decentralization of the government's extractive capacity during the transition period, which has increased the regressiveness of the regional fiscal pattern by reducing the central government's ability to redistribute resources from richer to poorer provinces. The second has to do with the regressive nature of net transfers between households, on the one hand, and state and collectives, on the other, as revealed by our surveys. We take these up in turn.

Weak and Decentralized Fiscal Capacity

Before the reform period began, the government obtained almost half of its revenues directly from the state-owned enterprises (SOEs), particularly those in light manufacturing industries. Government control of prices and wages and the absence of a competitive non-state sector enabled SOE profitability to be guaranteed. SOE profits became current revenue of the government, and this was used to fund new investment.

After the transition period began in the late 1970s, control over most product prices was gradually ended; wages and raw materials prices were raised; and a non-state sector grew up rapidly, consisting of TVEs, private firms, joint ventures of various kinds, and foreign-funded enterprises. Imports of consumer goods also poured into China. All this greatly increased competitive pressures on the SOEs, and their profitability quickly eroded. As its principal source of revenues dried up, the government failed to find new tax sources in the rapidly growing economy, and the share of government budget revenue at all levels in GDP fell from 35.8% in 1978 to only 11.2% in 1995. This is only slighly more than one-third the average of 32% for 22 developing countries whose data on general government expenditures are included in the IMF's *International Financial Statistics*.[15] About three-fifths of the drop was directly attributable to the fall in SOE contributions. Only when the fiscal system was restructured in 1994 to give greater weight to broad-based taxes (such as the value-added tax) did government's formal share of GDP slowly begin to recover, to 12% of GDP in 1997 and 12.5% in 1998.[16]

The formal budget, however, is not the only channel for government to obtain and use resources. As the formal budget declined relative to the economy, a wide variety of "extra-budgetary funds" of different kinds grew up to pay for various government services and programs. The principal components of extra-budgetary funds include fees collected by public institutions and agencies, township levies and village-retained funds, fees collected by local finance bureaus, and contributions to social insurance funds.[17] The second category, in particular, is used to support education, family planning, and local infrastructure, to pay village leaders and teachers, to give aid to poor households, and to invest in village businesses—in other words, to fund many of the activities crucial to local economic and social development.

Estimates of the size of extra-budgetary funds vary. Official Chinese estimates range from a "blue ribbon" government audit in 1996 that put them at 6% of GDP, to a range of 8–10% of GDP used by the

Ministry of Finance in 1998, to a figure of 15% of GDP mentioned repeatedly by the State Tax Administration in the same year.[18] Christine Wong, a close student of public finance in China, has made a comprehensive inventory of all such funds, including directed bank loans to SOEs (which alone averaged 6–8% of GDP during 1985–1995) and finds them to add up to between 16% and 24% of GDP. [19] Thus, extra-budgetary funds are sizable, amounting to at least half of formal budget revenues and perhaps as much as 200% of such revenues. If the upper-end estimates are anywhere near accurate, and especially if we include directed bank loans, we would have to conclude that the total of resources wielded by government, relative to GDP, has not really declined from its peak in the 1970s. Instead, much of this total has been decentralized to local governments and particular institutions and agencies and no longer comes under the unified control of the Ministry of Finance.

As we have seen, extra-budgetary funds are used to pay for some important and valuable public services and investments. Nevertheless, these funds suffer from several major shortcomings. First, having grown up piecemeal over two decades, they are poorly accounted for and weakly monitored at best. There is good reason to believe that they are undercounted, easily diverted from intended uses, and vulnerable to corruption. Moreover, their uses are not subject to any kind of unified evaluation of effectiveness relative to alternative ways of using the same resources.

Second, the decentralization of public finance of which extra-budgetary funds are the symbol is inherently regressive. Reliance on these resources increases with a decrease in administrative level and is most pronounced at the village level (not a formal government administrative level at all), which is almost entirely dependent on them. As Naughton (1999) explains:

> [E]xtra-budgetary funds are most significant precisely at those levels where formal revenue sources are least developed, and where needs and development levels vary the most. The result is that extra-budgetary funds contributed to interregional inequalities. Implicit tax rates from extra-budgetary revenues are certainly higher in poorer regions, and lower in more developed regions.

Moreover, the decentralized fiscal system does not allow fiscal transfers from richer to poorer regions and localities. "Each region is required to be more or less fiscally independent, tailoring its public expenditures to the revenues it can collect" (World Bank, 1997b, p. 27). As a result, there is a close correlation between regional per capita income and regional per capita government expenditures, which reinforces already wide inequalities in public spending on such crucial social services as health, education, and environmental protection.

The evaporation of fiscal transfers from richer to poorer provinces during the transition period is shown in Table 7.1, which reports average ratios of fiscal surplus (deficit) to GDP for China's thirty provinces at the beginning of the transition period and in 1990–1993.[20] When the transition was just starting, half of China's provinces had surpluses. Shanghai gave to the central government a surplus that came to over half of its GDP; and other developed provinces, including Beijing, Tianjin, and Liaoning also turned over large surpluses.[21] On the

TABLE 7.1. Ratio of Fiscal Surplus (Deficit) to GDP, by Province, 1978–1993 (Percent)

Region	1978–1980	1991–1993
Beijing	25.63	1.05
Tianjin	26.33	3.85
Hebei	6.00	0.10
Shanxi	−0.28	−0.82
Inner Mongolia	−20.77	−7.14
Liaoning	22.38	0.99
Jilin	−2.88	−3.66
Heilongjiang	−7.33	−1.71
Shanghai	51.07	8.54
Jiangsu	11.26	1.37
Zhejiang	6.98	2.03
Anhui	3.17	−2.30
Fujian	−1.38	−0.93
Jiangxi	4.48	−2.82
Shandong	10.18	−0.01
Henan	2.65	−0.61
Hubei	2.19	−0.30
Hunan	3.23	−0.56
Guangdong	4.76	0.38
Guangxi	−7.97	−2.25
Hainan	−3.14	−5.87
Sichuan	0.50	−0.84
Guizhou	−11.70	−3.34
Yunnan	−9.71	−1.19
Tibet	NA	−49.6
Shaanxi	−1.24	−2.44
Gansu	6.56	−3.83
Qinghai	NA	−11.57
Ningxia	−22.01	−10.17
Xinjiang	−24.15	−7.02

Source: Wang Shaoguang (1999), as incorporated in UNDP (1999b).

other hand, poor provinces—such as Ningxia, Guizhou, Inner Mongolia, and Xinjiang—received subsidies from the central government that ranged up to a quarter of their GDP. After 1980, both surpluses from rich province and subsidies to poor provinces evaporated. In 1991–1993, Shanghai was turning over only about 8.5% of its GDP to the center, and the newly rich province of Guangdong contributed a mere 0.4% of its GDP. As a result, the size of central subsidies to deficit provinces fell sharply.[22] Many poor areas have had difficulty financing basic services, such as education, and have no resources for investing in economic development.[23]

The third major problem with the decentralized fiscal system is that it tends to favor allocation of resources to uses that promise financial profit, such as TVE development, and it discriminates against social-sector spending, which—however important to social and economic development—does not yield immediate financial payoff. One result is that public spending on health has fallen sharply during the transition period: whereas 71% of the population had access to government health facilities in 1981, by 1993 only 21%—mostly in urban areas—still had such access (World Bank, 1997b, p. 25). The rural population was largely thrown back on its own resources for obtaining health care.[24]

The Chinese government has already recognized the need to bring better control to fiscal matters. In August 1996, for instance, it overhauled extra-budgetary funds, bringing thirteen major categories into the formal budget (Wang, 1999). It is likely that the budget share of GDP will increase as more extra-budgetary funds are brought within the budget, greater tax compliance is achieved, the many tax exemptions for domestic and foreign firms are eliminated, and new broad-based tax sources are found. From the perspective of stemming the tide of rising inequality in China, creating a capacity to use public resources more equitably is an urgent step that needs to be taken. Beyond this general structural reform, specific measures should be undertaken to promote greater regional equality; these would include directed credit to support "infant" enterprises in poor regions, and time-bound fiscal incentives to help foreign and domestic investors overcome the transitional disadvantage of locating in poor areas.

State-Household Fiscal Interaction

Data from our surveys also reveal highly regressive aspects of the fiscal system that make it disequalizing and aggravate poverty. The element of income that is under consideration consists of net transfer between households, on the one hand, and the state and collectives, on the other. For simplicity, we call this "net taxes" (if negative) or "net subsidies" (if positive). The usual reason that governments resort to a system of transfers is to improve the distribution of income. A targeted transfer to the poor—a higher than average rate of net subsidies, or a lower than average rate of net taxes for the poor—is often recommended and used as an instrument for improving the distribution of income and reducing the incidence of poverty. In China, however, this instrument has paradoxically aggravated both inequality and poverty.

In rural areas, the groups we have called the broad poor and extreme poor pay "net taxes" at rates that are, respectively, 27 and 36 times higher than the "net tax" rate paid by the non-poor (Table 7.2). Merely making these taxes proportional would improve the condition of the poor significantly. For example, the reduction of the tax rate on the broad poor to the rural average of 0.48% of income (from the existing 3.56%) would reduce the average income gap of those in poverty by 11%. The effect would be more dramatic if the net tax rate could be made progressive with, for example, a positive net transfer for the very poor.

In urban areas, the Gini ratio of income distribution rose from 0.233 in 1988 to 0.332 in 1995. Between these years, net subsidies to the households were drastically reduced, but the ones that were reduced included the most equalizing subsidies, ration-coupon subsidies. The remaining subsidies, dominated by in-kind housing subsidies, are highly disequalizing. As Table 7.2 shows, housing subsidies going to the non-poor, even as a share of their higher incomes, are well over twice the income share of housing subsidies going to the poor (and in

TABLE 7.2. Rural Net Transfer from (to) State and Collectives, and Urban Subsidies, 1995 (Percent of Total Income)

| | | Urban Transfers | |
	Rural Transfers	Housing Subsidy	Other Net Subsidies
Extreme poor	−4.66	4.42	0.96
Deep poor	−3.86	4.24	1.19
Broad poor	−3.56	3.84	1.25
Non-Poor	−0.13	9.89	1.25
Average	−0.46	9.74	1.25

Note: For definitions of extreme, deep and broad poor, see Chap. 4. A negative number denotes a net tax, i.e., a transfer from households to the state and collectives (see Chap. 1).

absolute terms, of course, the advantage of the non-poor is even greater). The weighted average concentration ratio for urban net subsidies is 0.492, well above the Gini ratio. Had the distribution of all net subsidies been just equal among all households on a per capita basis—that is, had their concentration ratio been zero—the Gini ratio of urban income distribution would have been 0.278 instead of 0.332. This would have reduced the incidence of urban poverty very substantially.

The regressively redistributive outcome of the fiscal system is perhaps the most outstanding anomaly of China's poverty alleviation strategy. It offsets much of whatever positive results might derive from the targeted interventions to reduce poverty. The reform of the fiscal system should be a matter of high government priority, even though any reform of its redistributive outcomes is unlikely to be politically or fiscally painless.

6. Urban Employment

Perhaps the most complex issues of China's current problem of inequality and poverty relate to the extreme employment hostility of urban growth. We have argued that, although in the long run it may prove to have been merely transitional, the period of transition has already been long enough to justify compensatory action. We would further highlight the importance of putting in place an adequate substitute before dismantling the system of social protection practiced in the past, which tolerated concealed unemployment in state and collective enterprises.

Compensatory public action must be designed on a broad front. There are three types of action that stand out as obvious candidates for high priority. The first is the institution of a transparent system of unemployment insurance. Estimates of real urban unemployment in 1998 reached 16 million, with millions more still on the job but with wages discontinued or reduced (Chap. 6). This number is expected to grow in the years immediately ahead if the government sticks to its announced intention to reform state enterprises. The prevalent view seems to be that the scope of any system of unemployment insurance must be limited, given the country's current level of development. In fact, the weight of opinion seems to favor concentrating the benefits of an unemployment relief system on older workers who have little chance of being reemployed and/or who are close to retirement. However, it is relevant to point out that laid-off workers were for years carried indirectly by the government through subsidies and politically directed bank loans to their enterprises. It would be far better to support them openly through government transfers; this would free both enterprises and banks from costs that impede their ability to embrace the market, and it would greatly increase the transparency of the operations of government, enterprises, and the banking system. Moreover—to underline the argument made in the previous section—this shift can be accomplished, if at all, only by replacing the current pernicious and easily abused system of relying on credit creation and various ad hoc extra-budgetary devices to accomplish government objectives. Instead, China needs to press on with a fiscal reform that will substantially increase budgetary tax revenues relative to GDP.

Second, an urban public works program of substantial magnitude, with a focus on the improvement of infrastructure, should be implemented as an immediate way of constructively absorbing unemployed workers. Third, a program of micro-enterprise development—combining the provision of training, credit, and technology—should be developed to encourage self-employment. These programs should be carefully designed to avoid an increase in the incentive for rural-to-urban migration. Thus, the wage rate in the public works program and the "subsidy" element in micro-enterprise development should be kept low.

Some action along these lines has already been taken. China is currently working to establish an unemployment insurance system. A program of training for the urban unemployed was instituted some years ago, along with the provision of placement services. These programs need to be strengthened and woven into a coherent overall policy to deal with urban unemployment comprehensively. Remedies must be found for the very limited availability of retraining facilities and labor market services. Many of the redundant workers need to acquire new skills before becoming eligible for reemployment, and most of the retrained workers need help from job placement agencies. Most important, perhaps, is the need for workers laid off by state enterprises to separate psychologically from their former work units, which were responsible for all elements of their well-being in the past, and become committed to seeking work elsewhere. This can happen only when the state takes over from the work unit the responsibility for basic pension provision, health insurance, unemployment insurance, and other aspects of social insurance in a dependable and adequately funded manner.[25]

In the aftermath of the Asian crisis of 1997, it is unlikely that external demand will continue to fuel China's growth at the same rate as in the past decade. To maintain its growth, China must therefore shift its emphasis to a relative stimulation of domestic components of demand. This creates both an opportunity and a necessity for an expansion of public works programs in productive capital construction. While it creates entitlements on the part of the poor, such a program can also be used to improve infrastructure in disadvantaged regions.

Although we have argued that the observed low output elasticity of employment is due mainly to the initial circumstances of surplus labor in state and collective enterprises, we have also pointed out that a process of capital deepening has been under way, with fixed assets of state enterprises increasing at well over twice the rate of increase of employment during 1990–1996.[26] Attention should be given to ensuring that the incentive system does not get distorted in the direction of promoting technologies that have a socially inappropriate degree of capital intensity. In the scramble for collaboration with foreign direct investors, the danger of indiscriminately adopting the technologies with which these investors are familiar is very real. Whatever the reasons for the recent trend of increasing capital intensity, it is important to ensure that strong pro-employment incentives be in place in an era of labor surplus.

7. Migration Policies

In Chapter 6 we discussed the adverse effect of China's residence permit (*hukou*) system, which strictly limits migration, on overall distribution of income and on poverty. It is understandable that Chinese policymakers do not want to risk the disorder that might follow a sudden and wholesale removal of these controls, but an orderly move away from this system is very important for both poverty alleviation and a more efficient system of labor allocation. In recent years, China has indeed made major de facto changes in its policy of restricting migration from rural to urban areas, and such migration has mushroomed. Available estimates suggest that about 8% of the rural labor force are away from home working or seeking work at any given time, but the number varies greatly by region, with poorer provinces furnishing the largest proportions of their rural labor force.[27] Over 10% of the rural work force in our sample reported leaving home to work or seek work during 1995.

The official poverty alleviation program encourages migration of workers out of ecologically fragile regions, although these programs have a strong preference for the relocation of the migrants in other rural areas and smaller towns and cities. Temporary residence permits are reported to have been given to many of the "floating" migrants in urban areas, while the presence of the remainder there has usually (but not always) been tolerated. Without these policies, the problem of poverty in China would have been more acute than it is.

Migrant laborers have often taken jobs that full-status urban residents are loath to fill—for instance, in heavy construction or what are regarded as menial service tasks. Often they have created their own jobs, bringing with them capital and skills—as in the case of fur and leather workers in Beijing's migrant community known as "Zhejiang Village." Operating in a segmented labor market, they were removed from direct competition for jobs with formal residents. However, with the growth of urban unemployment this segmentation has been breaking down, and migrants and regular residents increasingly find themselves competing for the same jobs. This has led to pressures for expelling migrants from cities or imposing various constraints on their ability to live and work in town. Such pressures should be resisted; instead, population mobility should be further liberalized. Existing migrants should be given residence permits to end the duality in the urban labor market, and they should progressively be entitled to the same services—from garbage collection to education and health care—as permanent residents. However, such liberalization of the labor market should go hand in hand with the measures discussed earlier to provide adequate help to the unemployed; otherwise, it can easily lead to serious conflict between established and migrant workers.

It should also be recognized that, with the growth of the market, physical restrictions are an increasingly ineffective method of stemming the flow of migration; this has been amply demonstrated by the large-scale circumvention of these restrictions in recent years. Physical restrictions on migration are a poor antidote to the incentives arising out of the numerous other physical interventions that have made the urban/rural income disparity in China one of the highest in Asia. Policies should concentrate on reducing the difference in earnings between rural and urban areas by shifting investment, jobs, and social spending to rural locations, and by reducing subsidies and benefits to which only urban employees are entitled. The policies recommended for an enhanced flow of resources to the rural economy, especially for the development of non-farm employment, and for keeping the rewards for urban workers realistic, should help in this regard. A major benefit of the urban residence permit has been the accompanying entitlement to heavily subsidized housing. An orderly elimination of this subsidy will both reduce the incentive of the rural population to migrate and enlarge the fiscal capability to undertake other urban programs for poverty reduction. As we saw in Chapter 3, such a housing reform has in fact made substantial progress, but in a manner that has unfortunately been highly disequalizing with respect to the distribution of income.

8. Targeted Support to the Poor

An important feature of China's official poverty reduction strategy is its rejection of a targeted income subsidy approach. According to information provided by the office of the Leading Group for the Development of Poor Areas, in 1995 the central government alone provided 10.8 billion yuan for poverty alleviation programs. This amount of resources could eliminate half of the extreme poverty in rural China, according to our estimates, and all the rural poverty according to official estimates, in a perfectly targeted program of income transfer.[28] Given that funds were also available from local government sources, as well as from international agencies and both foreign and domestic NGOs, a targeted income subsidy approach could have eliminated poverty, as officially defined, even after allowing for substantial leakage.

The reasons this did not happen are (1) the so-called poverty alleviation funds are often designated for productive investment rather than transfer; and, (2) China has rejected the policy of targeted income transfer. Whether the information base and the organizational capability of the government are adequate for the implementation of a reasonably well-targeted income subsidy program is something on which one must reserve judgment. What is known is that China's poverty reduction strategy rejects the income subsidy approach (the "relief approach") and instead focuses on the development of the capacity to produce income in poor areas. In implementing this approach, there is little or no targeting of poor households. The 8-7 Plan encouraged the creation of groups consisting of non-poor and poor—and led by the non-poor—to engage in income-enhancing activities in poor areas. That the gain made by the non-poor may exceed the gain made by the poor, both absolutely and in percentage terms, is not a consideration that discourages public support for projects of this kind. Both the overall development strategy and the direct poverty reduction programs in China seem to be premised on a strong endorsement of the "trickle-down" approach.

Chinese policymakers' rejection of targeted income subsidies is in part a reaction to the past "iron rice bowl" policy of extreme and inefficient egalitarianism through guaranteed income and employment. There is perhaps insufficient recognition, however, that a minority of the poor—especially poor households with a low labor endowment—cannot benefit significantly from most of the poverty reduction programs sketched above. The only way to pull such people out of poverty may be a targeted program of income subsidies. Even when the poor are in a position to benefit from income-enhancing development projects, these should be better targeted to poor households themselves. For instance, because the relevant policy bank, the ADB, has no presence below the county level, poverty alleviation loans have been administered for it by the Agricultural Bank of China (ABC), whose officers neither understand nor are motivated to implement anti-poverty policy loans.

It is particularly important to reverse the trend of reduced access of the poor to health and education services. Targeted intervention may be an effective method of dealing with this phenomenon. Once again, one can detect signs of change in the orientation of public policy. Recently the government has decided to establish a rural cooperative medical insurance system similar to that of the collective era. From the current 10% level, its coverage is planned to rise to 80% of the rural population by the year 2010.[29] This is intended to improve the access of the rural population, especially the poor, to health service.

9. Macroeconomic Policies and Implications

Many of these policies will divert resources away from capital accumulation to what is conventionally defined as consumption, although in each case we have emphasized the need to reduce the demand for resources. If these policies are implemented, China will find itself unable to continue to maintain as large a wedge between growth in GDP and growth in personal income as in the past. This would be good for future poverty reduction unless the rate of investment declines so substantially that it significantly reduces the rate of GDP growth.

Although the inexorable rise in the marginal saving rate will cease if these measures are implemented, there is no reason to believe that the average saving rate will decline (or decline significantly). After all, the improvement in the terms of trade for agriculture since 1994 has not led to a halt in the rise in the rate of accumulation. Several of the measures — e.g., the reduction of urban subsidies for the non-poor — should contribute to public savings. Moreover, many of the measures would enhance productivity and savings in the private sector. Finally, there is considerable room for China to swap its preoccupation with ever-increasing rates of accumulation for efforts to improve productivity of investment and efficiency of resource use. This objective gains even more importance from the extraordinary destruction of China's natural environment that has attended its race toward economic modernity—a subject we cannot explore in this monograph, despite its great significance.[30]

10. Implications for Globalization

A number of policies discussed above are aimed at offsetting the disequalizing forces that were unleashed at least partly by the process of globalization. This study argues that it is far more desirable to offset the adverse distributional consequences of globalization than either to ignore them or, alternatively, to abandon globalization and thereby lose the benefits of higher growth and greater efficiency that it brings.

The international aspect of China's integration with the world economy has consisted of a substantial liberalization of imports without compromising the ability of the country to support worthwhile infant industries, both in the domestic market and in the world market; it has also educed a greater respect for intellectual property. On the other hand, liberalization of the capital account has so far been rejected. China may have to make further concessions on trade liberalization and intellectual property rights in the process of negotiations for membership in the World Trade Organization (WTO). It appears unlikely, however, that in doing so China will cripple its ability to promote industries in which it believes it has a future (rather than a present) comparative advantage. Nor is it likely that China will face much pressure from the international community to liberalize its capital account. In the aftermath of the Asian crisis that began in 1997, the enthusiasm of the international community for capital account liberalization has waned. The World Bank, high priest of orthodoxy in the matter of development policy, has recently been urging caution in liberalizing capital accounts, and one of its recent reports argues that international experience shows no evidence that such liberalization enhances growth or that capital controls reduce growth.[31] Indeed, international experience in the 1990s points to the high risk of financial crises, often leading to years of negative growth and stagnation, to which countries subject themselves by dropping capital controls.

Maintaining a health rate of growth is a necessary condition for China to succeed in adequately reducing poverty. It is therefore important for China to maintain an architecture of globalization that will not put limits on its ability to grow rapidly. In this regard, it is necessary for China to continue both to maintain its ability to promote infant industries (including infant exports) and to protect itself from the volatility that governs international capital movement.

11. Conclusion

China does not have a policy of reducing inequality per se, and its policy for poverty reduction is segregated from the rest of its economic policies. The result is that many targeted actions for poverty reduction are offset or reversed by the adverse distributional consequences of overall economic policies, in the formulation of which distributional considerations do not seem to feature significantly. China's policy of eliminating poverty by improving the average incomes of designated poor counties both misses some very important poor groups that are located outside these counties and results in large leakages in the form of resource flows going to the non-poor in these counties. China should end the segregation of its poverty reduction strategy by making it an integral part of economic development strategy. The focus of targeted geographic interventions should be sharpened, and overall economic policies should be brought into consistency with the objectives of these interventions, so that policies to reduce inequality and poverty can operate in tandem on a broad front.

8

Summary and Conclusions

· ·

Unlike many other countries in transition from a régime of central planning to one of market coordination, China has experienced almost uninterrupted economic growth since its reforms began in the late 1970s. Between 1988 and 1995, the years of our two surveys, real per capita GDP increased at an annual rate of 8.1% per year—which amounts to an aggregate growth of 72% when compounded over seven years. Accumulated rapid growth has transformed the appearance of the country, especially the coastal cities and their surrounding farm belts. Changes have been qualitative as well as quantitative, with substantial shifts in popular attitudes and behavior, a proliferation of retail shops and restaurants, and a mushrooming of foreign direct investment and trade; the last has brought imported consumer durables, including all the accouterments of modern information technology.

However, China's unprecedented growth during this period was accompanied by a sharp increase in inequality. The result, as we have shown, is an unimpressive record of poverty reduction. The Head Count index of overall rural poverty declined by less than one-fifth, while there was actually an increase in rural poverty over much of the vast heartland of central China as well as in more remote and resource-poor regions. Overall urban poverty increased, and there were examples of increasing poverty even among the rich coastal provinces.

Part of China over these years linked itself to the world economy. That link had begun to be forged even before the beginning of the transition period in the late 1970s. Indeed, the rapprochement with the capitalist world and the global economy was actually initiated in the early 1970s, when China was still ruled by Mao Zedong, and from that time on trade relations developed steadily. However, it was very much a case of the Chinese dog wagging a global economic tail until the mid-1980s. Since then, China's exports as a proportion of GDP have more than doubled, and there has been a virtual explosion in the volume of FDI inflow into China.

It is our contention that the shift to a "coastal development strategy" in the mid-1980s, which connected China more closely with the world economy and attracted huge amounts of foreign direct investment, was also an important cause of the profound change in the relation of economic growth to income distribution and to poverty. Earlier fast growth had gone hand in hand with an egalitarian distribution, which became in some respects even more egalitarian in the early years of reform, and with a stunning decrease in absolute poverty. After the mid-1980s, however, continued rapid growth in GDP per capita was accompanied by an unusually rapid widening of income inequality in both rural and urban China, by a much retarded rate of poverty reduction in the countryside, and by a significant *increase* in absolute poverty in the towns and cities.

It is these latter trends associated with the "era of globalization" since the mid-1980s that we have tried to document in this book, whose empirical basis is the two national surveys of household income carried out in 1988 and 1995. We now summarize the main conclusions of this study and put them in the context of our argument.

1. Income Composition and Distribution

The trends at issue are closely linked to changes in the composition of income between the two survey dates. In the countryside, while household production activities—principally farming—remained the biggest single source of household income, their share of the total fell sharply, from 74% in 1988 to 56% in 1995.[1] The second largest rural income source, wages, advanced rapidly, from 9% of total income to 22%. Indeed, wages were the single fastest growing component of rural income in real terms.

The resulting change in the composition of rural income made it more unequal. The Gini ratio for rural income grew by 23%, from 0.34 to 0.42; virtually all of that increase was occasioned by the change in composition of rural income in favor of unequally distributed income sources, and very little of it by changes in distribution of the individual sources themselves. In other words, the faster-growing components of rural income were relatively unequally distributed, while the slow-growing ones were relatively equally distributed. For instance, wages, the fastest-growing income element, are the most important source of rural inequality, accounting for 40% of the rural Gini ratio in 1995. On the other hand, income from household farming activity, which grew very slowly and declined as a percentage of the total, is the most equalizing source of rural income, in the sense that its contribution to the rural Gini ratio is much smaller than its contribution to total rural income.

A particularly noteworthy aspect of rural distribution is the fact that the net transfer from households to the state and the collectives—embodying a positive rate of net "taxation"—has a highly disequalizing effect on rural distribution. The burden of net taxes is more than fully borne by the lower income groups: the top two deciles of the rural distribution are the only income groups that receive positive net transfer from the state and the collectives. The extreme regressiveness of the system of transfer indicates the neglect of income distribution considerations in public policy formation.

In the towns and cities, overall inequality increased even faster than in the countryside; the urban Gini ratio rose from 0.23 to 0.33, a 43% increase in just seven years. Unlike in the countryside, however, changes in the composition of urban income were not responsible for this rise in inequality. Rather, the cause was increasing inequality of distribution of the individual income components.

The largest source of urban income by far is wages, which increased their share from 44% to 61%. Income of retirees grew from about 7% to about 12% of income. Rental value of owner-occupied housing grew sharply, from less than 4% of income to over 11%, reflecting substantial progress in the housing reform as well as sharp increases in rents. However, housing was a major source of inequality: housing subsidies, though much reduced in 1995, became sharply more unequal, while the rental value of owned housing was the most disequalizing component of urban income in 1995; about three-fifths of privately owned housing assets belonged to the richest 10% of the urban population. The privatization of urban housing thus greatly exacerbated urban inequality.

There was a remarkable decline in other net subsidies, from over one-fifth of total urban income to only 1%. The fading away of urban subsidies, which are not included in the State Statistical Bureau's definition of income, is largely responsible for the much slower growth of urban income in our estimate than in that of the SSB. For the same reason, our estimates reveal no substantial increase in the average urban/rural income gap, whereas SSB's estimates show the gap to have risen substantially between 1988 and 1995. Another reason for this difference is that our rural income grows faster than SSB's because of our inclusion of such fast-growing income components as rental value of owner-occupied housing.

When rural and urban populations are considered together, the overall distribution of income exhibits greater inequality than either rural or urban income taken separately. This is true because the urban/rural income disparity dominates inequality within either population group. China's urban/rural gap is unusually large in the international comparative context, at least in part because of policies favoring the urban population and economy. Among these, the past strict prohibition on population movement is especially important, because this prevented residents of poorer rural areas from finding or creating income-earning opportunities in the towns and cities. The urbanization rate was artificially constrained and the urban/rural gap magnified. However, in contrast to the SSB, we find no significant change in this gap between the years of our surveys. The other aspect of spatial inequality that we examined—interprovincial inequality—did increase significantly and was an important source of growing inequality in China as a whole.

The increase in overall inequality between 1988 and 1995 is due mainly to the increasing importance of rural wage employment, on the one hand, and the increasing inequality of distribution of all urban income components, on the other. The aspects that we have been able to measure of the state's (and collective's) fiscal interaction with both urban and rural households are highly disequalizing and have exacerbated overall inequality. All urban income sources have a disequalizing effect on overall income distribution, and all rural sources except wages have an equalizing effect. Thus, any redistribution of income in favor of the rural population is very likely to reduce overall inequality.

2. Poverty

Our two surveys permitted us to make independent analyses of the incidence and characteristics of poverty in China, and our findings differ in several respects from the findings and claims of others, including the State Statistical Bureau and the World Bank. We calculate alternative poverty thresholds for both urban and rural China, based on minimum nutritional standards and reasonable assumptions about the cost of food and its importance in the market basket of the poor. We use these thresholds to estimate the relative incidence (Head Count index) of poverty, as well as the depth of poverty (Proportionate Poverty Gap) and the distributionally weighted depth of poverty (Weighted Poverty Gap) among the poor. These and other relevant procedures and the assumptions surrounding them are set out in detail in Chapter 4.

All rural poverty estimates fall between 1988 and 1995. On the basis of our preferred consumer price index, poverty by the broadest definition declined by 13%, while the most extreme category of poverty declined by 22%; these reductions are well below the ones that result from using the official CPI. In general, the deeper poverty was, the faster it declined, and depth of poverty and distribution of income among the poor both improved faster than the Head Count index. Thus, despite worsening of the income distribution for the rural population as a whole, it improved for the poor. However, a simulation exercise indicates that poverty reduction would have been far greater—a halving of the Head Count index—had inequality in rural China remained unchanged between 1988 and 1995.

Urban poverty was much less prevalent than rural poverty, as one would expect from the higher standard of living in towns and cities, but it was substantially greater than has commonly been claimed by the Chinese government and the World Bank. Moreover, the changes in urban poverty between 1988 and 1995 were opposite from those in rural poverty: urban poverty *increased* between the two surveys. All categories of urban poor grew in numbers and proportion of the urban population when our preferred CPI is used, with the most extreme category increasing fastest (by 145.5%), followed by "deep poverty" (86.4%) and "broad poverty" (19.4%). Using the official CPI, as well, both "deep" and "extreme" poverty increased (by 51.9% and 107.7%, respectively), while "broad poverty" remained essentially unchanged. Thus—unlike the rural situation, where the deeper the poverty was, the faster it diminished over time—in the urban case, the deeper the poverty was, the faster its incidence grew. And whereas the depth of rural poverty lessened and income distribution among the rural poor improved faster than the fall in the head count of rural poor, in the urban case both the depth of poverty and the income distribution among the poor worsened faster than the head count rate increased. Poverty was both growing and deepening in urban areas.

Increasing urban poverty has gone hand in hand with growing unemployment, and we here investigate the links between the two. We find that all categories of urban poor have significantly lower labor force participation rates. Whereas 8.5% of our overall urban labor force were unemployed (including those laid off from their jobs) during all or part of 1995, the unemployment rate (in this sense) was between

21% and 25% among the poor. Unemployment seems to have played an important role in the generation of poverty. Its expected growth in the immediate future is likely to make the problem of urban poverty more urgent. However, though poverty rates were twice as high among the unemployed as among the employed, the great majority of the unemployed — about 85% — were not poor.

Despite the increase in urban poverty, most poor in China — almost 90% in 1995 — are residents of rural areas, but they are not limited to remote peripheral areas, as is sometimes claimed. Except for a handful of coastal provinces, rural poverty is widely prevalent in most provinces for which we have information. Its incidence has been rising in several contiguous provinces of the central heartland. Nor is China's urban poverty a marginal phenomenon: its incidence is quite widespread, except in some rich coastal provinces, and there has been a sharp increase in the incidence of urban poverty in many parts of China.

3. Human Development and Inequality

Human Development Index

Human development, as measured by the Human Development Index (HDI) estimates for China's provinces, closely follows provincial per capita income. Provincial rankings by HDI and income per capita were closely correlated. The richer, more economically developed provinces also had higher HDI values. A more redistributive development strategy would make possible a greater separation between human development and economic growth, in the sense that the *range* of the HDI distribution numbers could be reduced by shifting some resources to the poorer provinces. China's government (through the budget) commands an unusually low share of GDP for public use — about 12%, compared to 17% for India and over 30% for the U.S. (see Chap. 7). If government extracted a reasonably larger share of GDP and used it to achieve more equal per capita spending on health and education among the provinces, for instance, HDI numbers of poor provinces would come closer to those of rich, even if the rank order remained unchanged. Another approach to improving poor provinces' human development record would be to reduce the urban bias in current and past social policy. A strategy that spread to the rural population some of the resources and benefits heretofore available only to urban dwellers would tend to reduce interprovincial variation in human development, because the more backward provinces of the interior are also the less urbanized ones.

Gender Inequality

The continued survival of gender inequality is borne out by our surveys, first in the unbalanced sex ratios of infants and young children in rural areas. Both our samples are consistent with published official statistics that show an excessive number of male infants and young children relative to female, a situation that suggests the practice of sex-selective abortion and other kinds of behavior reflecting male preference in the countryside.[2] Men constituted 70% of rural respondents who reported leaving home for more than a month to work or look for work in 1995. Accordingly, women have been left to do an increasing share of the farm work. As in 1988, rural women in 1995 had lower incomes in part because they were underrepresented in off-farm wage employment, the principal source of higher incomes in the countryside. This underrepresentation carries over to retirement status: fewer women are formally retired and receiving pensions. In addition, their wages in off-farm employment have, if anything, fallen relative to men's. In 1988, rural women were underrepresented in higher-paid occupations and those requiring more skill and education. The same remains true in 1995, but some gains and some losses have been made in the interim (see Table 5.4). Most notably, perhaps, at the top of the occupational hierarchy—owner or manager of an enterprise—women have apparently suffered a sharp decline, from 26% representation in the 1988 sample to only 8% in 1995.

Urban women make up a majority of the work force among office workers, unskilled workers, and "other." They exceed their overall share of urban employment among owners of private or individual enterprises (which are mainly very small and rudimentary in nature), professional workers, and skilled workers. They are badly underrepresented in top managerial positions, such as head of institution and division head. Earnings for urban women also tend to be below those for men: for most job categories, women received significantly less than men. Their relative deficit was particularly great in the case of overtime pay, "waiting for job" allowance, income from post-retirement job, income from second job, individual proprietor's income, and pensions.

We find that women were a preponderant majority of those unemployed throughout 1995 and a smaller majority of those unemployed for part of the year. Among the latter, women's duration of unemployment averaged about a third of the year, about 25 days longer than men's. We conjecture that the disappearance of the system of guaranteed lifetime employment, the rapid decay of the former enterprise-based pension and other social welfare systems in recent years, and the slowness with which new systems are being put in place could cause city dwellers to feel more dependent on family ties for security in old age—a development that would both threaten the recent decline in fertility rates and strengthen dormant male preference in the urban population.

Health Care

Since the beginning of the transition period in the late 1970s, the health status of the Chinese people has continued to improve in general and on average. The disappearance of the cooperative medical system in the countryside, however, and the shift in health policy from a public health and prevention orientation to one of fee-for-service and emphasis on treatment have threatened the maintenance of these gains. Nevertheless, health care seems to be still widely available and affordable. We find that although fully 88% of rural medical expenses in 1995 were paid out of pocket, the amounts were small relative to income, and that, perhaps as a result, household medical spending was almost independent of household per capita income.

In the cities, the differentiation of the economy is leading to a parallel differentiation in means of financing medical care, such that an increasing number of urban residents have to pay for it out of their own pockets. Between our two surveys, the average medical expense for urban sample residents increased more than twice as fast as nominal urban income per capita. Yet this expense in 1995 still came to only about 3% of urban per capita disposable income, and we could find virtually no effect of income on medical expenditures.

Thus, within both the rural and urban populations, increased income differentiation and the commercialization of medical care had not, by 1995, resulted in significant differentiation in household spending on medical care. Nevertheless, between urban and rural populations there was a large gap in both average income (2.4 to 1, by our estimate) and average spending on medical care (3.2 to 1). Moreover, the most dramatic differences in health status also follow the urban/rural divide, which thus looms large as the most basic cause of inequitable distribution of health care. This suggests that as China replaces the eroding system of work unit-based health care delivery in the public sector, it should step up efforts to reestablish a risk-sharing cooperative insurance system for financing rural health care, and to bring to the rural majority health resources closer in quantity and quality to those enjoyed by the urban population.

4. Explanations

In trying to explain the increase in inequality and decline in poverty reduction during the period under study, we focused first on the wedge that opened between growth of GDP and that of personal income, which is the relevant variable for studying poverty. Changes in the poverty rate are determined by the growth in per capita personal income (not GDP) and the change in its distribution. Personal income grew much more slowly than GDP, and its lag explains part of the lackluster performance in poverty reduction. Had a larger part of the growth in GDP been passed on to households as rising personal income, China's poverty reduction record would have been better.

The policies responsible for this wedge were driven primarily by the constant upward pressure on investment and savings inherent in the structure of China's political economic system. "Investment hunger," especially by the local governments that have wielded increasing authority through the 1980s and 1990s, has been a core characteristic of the Chinese economy. The domestic savings rate reached a staggering 42% of GDP in 1995 (although an improved estimate of GDP would reduce this rate a bit). In our view, the government tried to rely on the fastest possible growth as its chief means of dealing with the increasingly complex problems of the transition—for example, the threat of rising unemployment from reforming state enterprises. Unwilling to restrict credit available to local governments, the state allowed an expansion of credit to pump up accumulation and drive a wedge between growth of GDP and that of personal income.

Nevertheless, the annual growth rates of personal income between 1988 and 1995—even if below those of GDP—were still very substantial, at 4.7% and 4.5% for rural and urban China, respectively. Indeed, had both rural and urban income distribution remained the same in 1995 as in 1988, then half of rural poverty and virtually all urban poverty would have been eliminated. Thus, it is the sharp rise in inequality that must shoulder much of the responsibility for China's pedestrian performance in reducing the incidence of poverty.

An important countervailing force to widening inequality deserves attention: the extraordinary equality of land distribution in rural China, which lies behind one of the few positive trends in the income distribution picture in rural China. By 1995, the concentration ratio for land had dropped to zero or close to zero, indicating that land was almost equally accessible to all income groups. This equality of access to land has been the main reason that income from farming is the most equalizing component of income in rural China.

There have been many calls for clarifying property rights in land or moving entirely to private ownership in order to improve farmers' incentives to invest in their land and preserve its fertility. The government has been sensitive to this argument, and in 1993 it decided that new land contracts should guarantee farmers' access to the land for 30 years, during which period no land adjustments should occur.[3] This policy seems to have been very unevenly carried out, and there is some evidence that many farmers prefer the more flexible arrangements that existed before because they support the principle of equal access and want to be able to exploit it when their own families grow.[4] Indeed, the existing arrangements have some powerful accomplishments to their credit: a very large increase in output and yields over almost two decades; avoidance of the growth of landlessness and the abject poverty that often accompanies it elsewhere in the developing world; provision of basic food security and income to the rural population; assurance of gender equality in access to land for subsistence grain production;[5] and, as we have seen above, an equalizing force on the income distribution in an otherwise rapidly polarizing scene. In our judgment, any change in the land tenure system should be based on a full consideration of its probable impact on all these important properties.

The single most important source of increased rural inequality in China during the period under review was unequal access to wage income, which was in turn fundamentally due to regionally unequal growth of off-farm employment opportunities. Unlike farm income, income from wages is a highly disequalizing component of rural income. Between 1988 and 1995, not only did wages became more unequally distributed, but their share in rural income also increased sharply. This implies that wages grew faster than rural income as a whole, but that wage-earning opportunities did not spread out from their initial bases. In criticizing this record, we do not seek to limit the growth of off-farm wage employment, but rather to bring public policy to bear in vigorously encouraging the spread of wage employment opportunities to poorer areas of the countryside through infrastructure development and investment in human capital and research and development, as well as through removing remaining impediments to the "opening up" of such regions to the global economy.

In urban areas, policymakers clearly hoped that labor-intensive industrialization would rapidly expand employment, offset the growing inequality of wage distribution, and prevent a rise in urban poverty. However, while employment rose briskly in construction, transport, trade and services, official statistics show industrialization so far to have been quite employment-hostile. Contrary to the theoretical expectation that freer trade, and the resultant greater integration with the world economy should increase the employment intensity of growth, and despite considerable evidence that rapidly growing export industries have indeed been labor-intensive, the output elasticity of employment in China's secondary industries fell drastically.[6]

The reason for this seems to be that, under increasing market pressure, state and collective enterprises began to reduce the "disguised unemployment" that they had maintained in the past under the policy of guaranteed employment. Once the transition has been completed and the concealed unemployment eliminated, China's industries should become more efficient and the observed output elasticity of employment should rise. But the very slow growth of industrial employment during the transition itself prevents the benefits of growth from spreading among broader sections of the population, with consequent adverse effect on inequality and the incidence of poverty. This has become an acute problem at present as the reform of state enterprises is leading to the disgorging of millions of their employees. The actual unemployment rate in 1995 has been estimated at 4.4–5.0% (compared with the published rate of 2.9%); by 1998, it had risen to between 7.9% and 8.5% (UNDP 1999b). Our analysis showed rising unemployment to be a potent contributor to rising urban poverty.

In attempting to explain the recent sharp upward trend in inequality, we must not neglect public finance. Those aspects of public finance that we were able to capture in our surveys show it to be quite regressive. For instance, although urban subsidies have fallen sharply in recent years, surviving net subsidies mainly benefit higher income groups. In recent years, there has been a substantial reduction of access of the poor to basic education and health resources. This is explained by the broad changes that have taken place in the arena of public finance during the transition era.

The most significant such change has been the continuous decentralization in public finance relative to GDP. This came about largely because of a fall in tax payments by state enterprises, whose profits were decimated by price reform and intensifying competition from other sectors, and the de facto replacement of these declining budget revenues with various extra-budgetary funds, largely at the provincial and local levels. These are very problematic substitutes for tax-based budget revenues, for reasons discussed in Chapter 7. Not only do they lend themselves to various abuses, but they have also greatly weakened the center's ability to redistribute resources in favor of more backward regions, as in the past, with the result that poorer regions and localities have had great difficulty financing basic public services, let alone infrastructure development or poverty alleviation programs.

5. Implications for Policy

In our summary of trends and explanations, it has proved impossible to refrain altogether from drawing various policy implications. Now we try to summarize, briefly but more systematically, the principal approaches to policy that seem desirable in the light of our analysis.

The key, in our view, is to promote a comprehensive strategy for reduced inequality and poverty that includes consistent actions involving both macroeconomic and institutional policies that influence the overall pattern of development, as well as microeconomic interventions to improve household capabilities. The government should incorporate analysis of income distribution and poverty implications into the planning process for all relevant policies and strategies. As we pointed out in the previous chapter, fostering growth through policies that channel resources away from poor areas and people and then trying to compensate via a poverty alleviation program turns out to have been an ineffective overall strategy for coping with poverty; and implies that the government's social welfare function assigns too low a de facto weight to poverty reduction. China, whose anti-poverty approach has been entirely focused on a limited number of designated poor counties, needs to formulate a comprehensive strategy that embraces rural poverty outside the designated counties as well as growing poverty in urban areas.

Because the great majority of the poor reside in the countryside, China cannot win its war against poverty, in general, without a decisive strategy for the reduction of rural poverty. A strategy to accomplish this should begin with an attack on the unusually large ratio of urban to rural income — one that reached almost 2.5 in 1995, compared with a ratio well below 2 in most developing Asian countries.

Policies that would bolster the relative position of the rural sector include the following:

1. Allow the terms of trade of this sector to be determined by economic forces without depressive public intervention. Despite substantial liberalization of farm prices and sharp increases in the mid-1990s, grain prices are still subject to considerable state control. The ending of such controls would further improve agriculture's terms of trade,

and have the added benefit of raising income in poorer central and western provinces that have a comparative advantage in grain production.

2. Improve the rural sector's share of public resources, including resources for health care, education, agricultural research and development, and infrastructure. A range of pressing rural needs requiring a stepped-up public role are mentioned in Chapter 7, from resolution of the severe water shortage in North China to encouragement of farming techniques that are more sustainable over the long run than those currently in use.

3. Promote rural non-farm activities. Such activities, including off-farm wage employment, have been an essential ingredient in the escape from poverty for many, and they should be strengthened within the limits of the actual and/ or potential comparative advantage of particular areas for these activities. Credit, technical knowledge, marketing facilities, and investment in infrastructure and education are all needed to make feasible the development of healthy linkages between the economies of poor areas and the rapidly growing coastal provinces.

4. Liberalize control of population movement so as to permit a freer flow of people in search of economic and social opportunity. We have argued that liberalized policies toward population mobility have helped reduce rural poverty, and we favor furthering this process—including the phasing out of physical restrictions on population movement—to eliminate the inequitable segmentation of the urban labor market and the second class status of rural–urban migrants. The best way to moderate the rural–urban population flow is to concentrate on reducing China's extreme urban/rural income gap by shifting investment, jobs and social spending to rural locations and by reducing subsidies and benefits that accrue only to urban residents. Yet it is important that all of this be done in the context of a vigorous program of the kind outlined below to help the urban unemployed; otherwise, it is likely to create dangerous tensions between "full-status" residents and migrants in the competition for scarce urban jobs.

Regional disparities in China have grown not only because of the natural advantages of relatively developed coastal provinces, but also because of various kinds of political and administrative discrimination against the poorer areas. All such discrimination should be discontinued.

The government's fiscal decline and the fiscal decentralization of the reform period have greatly reduced the contribution of China's fiscal system to spatial redistribution. Investment in infrastructure and in provision of education and health resources has been concentrated in richer regions. This needs to be addressed by means of a combination of measures, beginning with vigorous enhancement of the government's fiscal capacity and its use to effect spatial redistribution, and also including directed credit to support infants enterprises in poor regions, and redirection of public investment for infrastructure development. Appropriate fiscal incentives should be offered to foreign and domestic investors to help them overcome the transitional disadvantage of locating in poor areas.

Ordinarily, government transfers of income are recommended in order to help the poor or other relatively disadvantaged members of society; however, our estimates show that the fiscal interaction of households with state and collective is very regressive. For instance, what we have called the broad poor and extreme poor in the countryside pay "net taxes" at rates that are, respectively, 27 and 36 times higher than the "net tax" rate paid by the non-poor (Table 7.2). If this tax rate on the broad poor were merely lowered to the rural average rate, the average income gap of those in poverty would fall by 11%. Of course, the effect would be more dramatic if the net tax rate could be made progressive with, for example, a positive net transfer for the very poor.

In the towns, many relatively equally distributed subsidies have been rapidly eliminated, leaving behind subsidies that are very unequally distributed, especially the housing subsidy. Ordinarily, subsidies would be expected to have negative concentration ratios, since they are aimed at the poorer members of society. If all net urban subsidies were merely distributed equally among all urban households — that is, if their concentration ratio were zero — the Gini ratio of urban income distribution would fall from 0.33 to 0.28, which would substantially reduce the incidence of urban poverty.

The regressively redistributive outcome of the fiscal system is perhaps the outstanding anomaly in the effort to reduce poverty and inequality in China. It directly contradicts the goals of the poverty alleviation program. The sharp decline in China's formal budget relative to GDP has created a condition of permanent fiscal stringency in poor localities and has fostered inequitable distribution of fiscal resources over the provinces and localities. Reform of the fiscal system should be a matter of high priority and is in many ways prerequisite to other reforms needed to combat poverty and inequality.

The employment-hostility of recent urban growth, although transitional, is contributing to the growth of urban poverty and calls for compensatory action. The previous system of social protection, which was to tolerate concealed unemployment in state and collective enterprises, is being dismantled before an adequate substitute is put in place. Certainly, it is better to support unemployed workers openly through government transfers, retraining programs, and so on, thus freeing both enterprises and banks of costs that impede their ability to use the market effectively, as well as greatly increasing the transparency of the operations of government, enterprises, and the banking system. However, that support should be real and comprehensive. The completion of a transparent system of unemployment insurance is now a high priority. The situation also calls for an urban public works program which focuses on improvement of infrastructure, as well as a program of micro-enterprise development to encourage self-employment. Such programs should be carefully designed to avoid an increase in the incentive for rural–urban migration. Finally, care should be taken to avoid inappropriate incentives that lead to capital-deepening investments, which would further reduce the employment intensity of GDP growth.

In addressing the rural poverty alleviation effort, we recommend adjusting the current "trickle-down" approach by recognizing the need for direct income subsidies for some poor households and individuals who are unable to benefit from general regional development programs, and we call for better targeting of the programs to ensure that they reach more poor households. It is particularly important to reverse the trend of reduced access of the poor to health and education services. Targeted intervention may be an effective method of dealing with this phenomenon. The government's plan to rebuild a rural cooperative medical insurance system similar to that of the past is a hopeful sign that the access of the poorer rural population to health services will improve. Aside from some piecemeal programs, however, we are not aware of an effective overall response to the serious problem of education funding and access in poorer rural areas.

The balance of policy approaches advocated here would tend to lower China's extraordinarily high marginal savings rate, as well as to reduce the wedge between growth of GDP and that of personal income. We think this is all to the good. Healthy economic growth certainly can ease the problem of funding well-designed social programs, but headlong growth is not a substitute for such programs. Moreover, there is considerable room for China to replace its preoccupation with an ever-increasing rate of accumulation with efforts to improve productivity of investment and efficiency of resource use. In "growing out of the plan" (to use Barry Naughton's felicitous phrase), China's transitional economy cannot simply grow out of its problems of poverty and increasing inequality. A development strategy that embodies effective programs for addressing these ills is one that will also enhance stability and promote more sustainable development in the longer run.

Notes

· ·

Chapter 1

1. These growth rates are based on the data in World Bank, 1995a, 1997f.

2. These ratios are based on the official data on urban and rural personal incomes reported in State Statistical Bureau (SSB), 1996. As we shall argue later, the SSB estimates of personal income are biased owing to the exclusion of several important components; however, this does not affect the conclusion that urban/rural income inequality declined sharply in the early years of reform.

3. SSB, 1995. As will be discussed later, the extent of rise in this ratio turns out to be somewhat different once one accounts for personal income more comprehensively than the SSB does. The general conclusion, however, remains unchanged.

4. The ratio was 2.47 in 1995 and 2.27 in 1996, according to the SSB definition. See SSB, 1997.

5. World Bank, 1997b, p. 91.

6. World Bank, 1997f. "Low-income countries" is a World Bank classification which puts in this category all countries with a per capita GNP of $765 or less in 1995, according to the Bank's "Atlas Method." China belongs to this group. "Middle-income countries" are those which in 1995 had a per capita GNP of more than $765 but no more than $9,385.

7. See World Bank, 1998. The estimate for 1995 is not available.

8. For an analysis of the factors behind the shift in China's development strategy in the mid-1980s, see Khan, 1996.

9. Thus, for example, during the two-year period 1993–1995, the rate of saving was 41.5% of GDP, compared to the rate of investment of 41.2% of GDP. See World Bank, 1997f, for these estimates. Data from the same source indicate that the relative magnitudes of saving and investment rates were similar in other years.

10. The 1985 figure is from Asian Development Bank, 1993; the 1995 figure is from World Bank, 1997f. The increase in China's international reserves has continued after 1995; by early 1999 it had reached $149 billion.

11. See Riskin, 1987, for a discussion of this tendency.

12. The data on the trend in inequality have been discussed in Khan et al., 1992; the estimated trend in poverty is reported in World Bank, 1992b.

13. These again are documented in Khan et al., 1992, and World Bank, 1992b.

14. For example, Ravallion and Chen, 1998, makes an interesting analysis of the effect on the estimates of inequality of using different rates of price increase for different provinces.

15. The term "household income" is used in this study interchangeably with the more commonly used term "personal income."

16. Main results were first published in Khan et al., 1992, and a longer version was included in Griffin and Zhao, 1993. The method adopted by the survey is discussed in Marc Eichen and Zhang Ming, "The 1988 Household Sample Survey—Data Description and Availability," in Griffin and Zhao, 1993. The methodology was substantially the same for the survey repeated for 1995.

17. In the past, China strictly regulated rural–urban migration by requiring every household residing in a particular locality to obtain an official residence permit, without which access to numerous entitlements—e.g., ration coupons, housing, entry to educational institutions, and use of health facilities—were denied. In recent years, large-scale migration without residence permits has been tolerated, although the migrants have continued to be excluded from access to public housing, education, health, and other urban public services.

18. As stated above, the results of the 1988 survey are reported in Khan et al., 1992 and 1993, and in Griffin and Zhao, 1993.

Chapter 2

1. To those who might be hesitant about the need to estimate the rental value of housing in this indirect way, we would like to argue as follows. First, it is a standard international practice in income accounting to include the rental value of owned housing. Second, in the rural areas of developing countries, without a significant rental market for housing, the common practice is to estimate rental value according to indirect methods similar to the one that we have employed. The consequence of excluding the rental value of owned housing can be gauged by considering a person who—because of a change in the location of employment, for example—moves out of her owned home into a rented house of exactly similar proportions and rents out her own home for an amount that exactly equals the rent she herself now pays. If rental value of owned housing were excluded, then, *ceteris paribus*, this move would make her richer, although in fact she is exactly as well off as before!

2. It may be noted that in 1988, market rent was estimated indirectly, first by indirectly estimating the replacement value of the house, and, next, estimating market rent as 8% of the replacement value. See Griffin and Zhao, 1993, Chap. 1.

3. We do not have separate estimate of farm income for 1988. This consists of the sum of the gross value of self-consumption of farm products and the net value of sale of farm products (which could not be separated from the net value of sales of non-farm products because of lack of details about inputs). Of the two, the gross value of self-consumption of farm products alone accounted for 41% of rural income in 1988, strongly suggesting that total farm income as a proportion of total income was far above 46%, the ratio for 1995.

4. Ideally, one should measure a "constant-utility price index" rather than a "constant-bundle-of-goods price index," of which both Laspeyre and Paasche indices are examples. Usually, the Paasche index understates the rate of increase in the constant-utility price index (for given utility in current year), while the Laspeyre index overstates the constant-utility price index (for given utility in base year). For a demonstration, see Allen, 1975.

5. What we have is (CPI for 1995/the CPI for 1988). For rural China this gives us:

$$\frac{\sum P^{95}Q^{95}/\sum P^{85}Q^{95}}{\sum P^{88}Q^{88}/\sum P^{85}Q^{88}}$$

whereas we want (if we are measuring the Paasche index),

$$\sum P^{95}Q^{95}/\sum P^{88}Q^{95}$$

or (if we are measuring the Laspeyre index)

$$\sum P^{95}Q^{88}/\sum P^{88}Q^{88}.$$

As is easy to see, there is no a priori basis to argue what relationship the "indices" shown in Table 2.2 (i.e., the values of the CPIs estimated by the SSB for 1995 as indices of their values in 1988) have to Paasche or Laspeyre indices of consumer prices for 1995 with 1988 as base. There is no simple way to conceptualize the indices shown in Table 2.2. Had the CPI of the SSB been based on the Laspeyre method, this would have a clear meaning; namely the proportionate change in expenditure between 1988 and 1995 on the given bundle of 1985 goods:

$$\frac{\sum P^{95}Q^{85}/\sum P^{85}Q^{85}}{\sum P^{88}Q^{85}/\sum P^{85}Q^{85}} = \sum P^{95}Q^{85}/\sum P^{88}Q^{85}$$

It is, of course, possible that it would still be a biased estimate of the desired constant utility CPI.

6. A disequalizing component contributes a higher proportion to the Gini ratio of income distribution than its share of total income. The Gini ratio (G) is the weighted average of the "concentration ratios" of the distribution of

individual components of income (C_i for the i-th component), weights being the shares of components in total income (q_i for the i-th component): $G = \Sigma q_i C_i$. The concentration ratio is calculated in the same way as the Gini ratio, except that the so-called Lorenz distribution for the i-th component from which it is estimated shows the cumulative shares of i accruing to cumulative proportions of individuals who are ranked in ascending order of *per capita income*, not per capita values of i. More on this in the next chapter.

7. This is estimated as the weighted sum of the 1988 concentration ratios, the weights being the income shares of the components in 1995. This issue is further elaborated in the next chapter.

8. The SSB has two different concepts of urban income, "per capita income" and "per capita income available for living" (see SSB, 1996, Table 9-5). From the meager explanation of concepts provided by the SSB, it is impossible to know what the difference between them is. In a table of comparative urban and rural per capita incomes, the SSB shows the latter of the two urban measures along with "per capita net income of rural households," suggesting that the two are comparable (SSB, 1996, Table 9-4). After a careful comparison of components, we have decided that "per capita income" is the relevant measure of income which has been used throughout as representing the SSB estimate.

9. The SSB estimates are 0.6% of income in 1988 and 2.4% in 1995, both somewhat below ours. This is surprising, since our estimates of income, the denominator, are substantially higher than SSB's.

10. The weighted average of the 1988 concentration ratios, weights being the 1995 income shares of components, gives an estimated urban Gini ratio of 0.238, compared to the 1988 Gini ratio of 0.233. This is discussed more fully in the next chapter.

11. The statement that SSB evidently excludes these items is based on both the lack of any explicit mention of them in SSB, 1997, p. 313, and the close similarity between SSB's estimate for "laborers' remuneration" and ours for regular plus non-regular wage income. We include pensions in wage-type income, whereas SSB probably includes them in transfers. It is possible that some or all of our additional categories are indeed included in "laborers' remuneration," in which case there is an inexplicably large gap between the respective estimates.

12. The saving rate for rural China was 17% (on the basis of the data in SSB, 1996, p. 300) and for urban China 17.5% (on the basis of the data in SSB, 1996, p. 284). Aggregate household incomes in urban and rural China are roughly equal, so that the weighted average saving rate is 17.25%. GNP estimate is also from SSB, 1996.

13. World Bank, 1997f.

14. The estimates for these other Asian countries are from World Bank, 1997f. There is, of course, the question whether the rates elsewhere are accurately estimated.

15. This is based on the data in SSB, 1996.

16. The annual growth rate in real per capita household income for China as a whole (the weighted average of rural and urban incomes) was higher than either the rural or the urban real income growth because there was a rise in the weight of the urban population, the richer of the two income groups, between 1988 and 1995.

17. See Khan et al., 1992, for evidence up to late 1980s, and the next chapter for evidence of change between 1988 and 1995.

Chapter 3

1. Thus, the Theil index, which, unlike the Gini ratio, can be decomposed, is sensitive to the sample size and is not amenable to an intuitive interpretation, which one can make of the Gini ratio. The Atkinson index is very sensitive to the subjective parameter representing degree of inequality aversion, which must be chosen arbitrarily. Estimates of none of these other indices are nearly as widely available, for purposes of comparison, as is the Gini ratio. For a comparison of different measures of inequality, see Sen, 1997.

2. The Lorenz distribution represents a function $L(x)$ which is the proportion of total income received by the lowest x proportion of income recipients. Its properties include: (a) $L(x) = 0$ for $x = 0$; (b) $L(x) = 1$ for $x = 1$; (c) $L(x) \leq x$; (d) $L'(x) > 0$; and (e) $L''(x) \geq 0$. The pseudo-Lorenz distribution satisfies properties (a) and (b), but not (c), (d), and (e). Thus, the concentration ratio is not bound by the limits of 0 and 1 that bind the Gini ratio. For the application of this method of decomposing the Gini ratio, see Fei, Ranis, and Kuo, 1978; Kuo, Ranis, and Fei, 1981; Fields, 1980; and Kakwani, 1980, 1986. Various names have been given to the indices showing the distributions of individual components of income. Kuo, Ranis, and Fei, 1981, call them "factor Gini ratios" (or simply "Gini ratios"); Fields, 1980, uses the name "pseudo-Gini coefficients"; and Kakwani, 1980, 1986, calls them "concentration indices." Fields, 1980, is a useful source for further explanation of the method and for reference to other applications of this kind of decomposition of the Gini ratio.

3. Decile shares of 1988 income and its components are shown in Khan et al., 1993.

4. Like most other users of Gini ratios, we have not tried to measure their standard errors. We have adopted the convention of designating any change in Gini ratio of 10% or greater as significant, but we cannot establish statistically the significance of a 10% difference or, indeed, of a larger difference, for that matter. We believe the plausibility of individual estimates of increased inequality is enhanced by the broad range of such increases, and by the meagerness of examples of counter movements. Readers are of course free to arrive at their own judgments.

5. See Khan et al., 1993, for comparative data for other Asian countries.

6. This pattern and its exacerbation by fiscal decentralization are discussed by Wong, Heady, and West, 1997.

7. Throughout this study, a change in the inequality of distribution of a component of income is measured by a change in its concentration ratio, not by a change in its Gini ratio.

8. Decile shares of urban income and its components for 1988 are shown in Khan et al., 1993.

9. See Guowuyuan Yanjiushi Ketizu (Study Group of State Planning Commission Research Office), 1997, in *Jingji Yanjiu*, no. 8, August 1997, p. 3.

10. We do not take the position that ration coupons, with their allegedly adverse consequences for efficiency, should have been retained. The point is that they were not replaced by alternative measures to offset the adverse distributional consequences of their abolition.

11. Estimates of both housing subsidies and rental value of owned housing depend on respondents' estimates of the market rental value of their homes. Whether housing markets are sufficiently developed in urban China to permit such estimates to be accurate is an open question. Subjective estimates might err considerably. For instance, our conclusions would be threatened if rental values were systematically overestimated, since this would raise the weight of their concentration ratios in the overall Gini ratio. If physical housing assets are concentrated among richer groups, then systematic exaggeration would also increase the concentration ratio of implicit rental income. We cannot think of any obvious reason why respondents would systematically exaggerate the rental value of their homes.

12. If property income is underestimated, as we earlier suggested it might be, then the Gini ratio is also (perhaps only slightly) underestimated, since property income is such a disequalizing source of income.

13. The other two components that became mildly more (less) equalizing (disequalizing) between 1988 and 1995 are cash income of retirees and miscellaneous income (private transfer and other unspecified sources).

14. In 1995 rural China represented 71% of total population of China. The share of rural population in the survey was just under 62%. We therefore drew a 50% random sample of rural households in the sample and added it to the sample. This raised the share of rural population in the survey to about 71%.

15. Decile shares of income and its components for 1988 are shown in Khan et al., 1993.

16. International comparison of Gini ratios is subject to many problems. One has to be particularly careful about the variable for which it is measured. Gini ratio of the distribution of per capita expenditure is typically lower than the Gini ratio of the distribution of per capita income. The Gini ratio of per capita income distribution in Pakistan was 0.407 in 1990–1991 (Amjad and Kemal, 1996). The Gini ratio of expenditure distribution for India (1992) was 0.338, and for Indonesia (1993) 0.317 (World Bank, 1997f). It is highly implausible that the Gini ratios for income distribution in India and Indonesia would be so much higher than their Gini ratios for expenditure distribution

as to be anywhere near China's Gini ratio. For the Philippines, the Gini ratio of distribution of expenditure was 0.43 (Balisacan, 1996).

17. See World Bank, 1997f. Unpublished official estimates for 1994, made by the Macroeconomics Institute of the State Planning Commission, were available to us at the time of writing. Their estimated Gini for personal income in 1994 was 0.434, very close to our own estimate for 1995. Their estimate for rural income was 0.411, again close to our own; for urban income it was 0.377, well above our estimate (personal communication from State Planning Commission, Department of Social Development, November 1997).

18. See Khan et al., 1992.

19. The index of terms of trade (the ratio of farm and sideline product price to rural retail price of industrial products) increased by 4.5%. Gross value of agricultural production increased by 10.9%. These data are from SSB, 1996.

20. See Khan, et al., 1992.

21. The standard deviation of rural provincial per capita income rises by 3.5 times, while the mean doubles.

22. The term "coastal provinces" refers to the eleven coastal provinces and Beijing, which derived the greatest benefit of China's integration with the global economy.

Chapter 4

1. These results are reported in World Bank, 1992b. The extraordinarily low urban poverty according to these World Bank estimates is due to the use of a very low poverty threshold for urban China, 30% below the actual expenditure on food alone for the poorest 5% of the urban households. See Khan, 1996, Annex.

2. These estimates, and the methodology underlying them, have been reported in Khan, 1996.

3. These indices are defined as follows:

$$\text{Head Count index: } HC = h/n$$

where h = the number of persons belonging to households with per capita incomes below poverty threshold in terms of income), and n = total population.

Proportionate Poverty Gap index (PPG):

$$PPG = (1/n) \sum_{i=1}^{h} [(PIT - Y_i)/PIT] = [\sum_{i=1}^{h} (PIT - Y_i)]/[n(PIT)]$$

$$= (h/n)(1/h) \sum_{i=1}^{h} [(PIT - Y_i)/PIT] = (HC)(I)$$

where I = average of the poverty gaps (i.e., proportionate income shortfalls) of the poor only.

The "Weighted Poverty Gap" index (our alternative to the more usual, if unmanageable, name "Foster-Greer-Thorbecke P_2 measure of poverty"), is defined as the mean of squared proportionate poverty gaps:

$$WPG = (1/n) \sum_{i=1}^{h} [(PIT - Y_i)/PIT]^2$$

The squaring of the proportionate poverty gap is a special formulation of the more general case of raising it to a non-negative power α. With α replacing 2, the measure represents a generic class of poverty indices. For $\alpha = 0$ the measure collapses to the HC index and for $\alpha = 1$ it becomes the PPG index.

4. The differences in the *levels* of head count poverty as estimated by the World Bank and Khan, 1996, are due to the differences in the poverty thresholds that have been used in the two studies. Khan, 1996, also uses a relatively much higher poverty threshold for urban China than for rural China. More is said later on the *level* of the poverty threshold.

5. Until very recently, the official view was that poverty in China was a rural phenomenon.

6. According to the SSB, the proportion of rural population in poverty fell from 31% in 1978 to 15% in 1984, remained almost unchanged thereafter until 1987 (14%), and then began to fall again (to become 7% in 1995). According to the SSB, 11% of the rural Chinese were in poverty in 1988. Thus, according to the SSB, the Head Count index of rural poverty declined by 36% between 1988 and 1995.

7. The implicit consumer price index (CPI) underlying SSB's poverty threshold was lower than the rural CPI for the years between 1985 and 1988 but higher than the rural CPI for the period between 1988 and 1995.

8. The World Bank continues to take the view that urban poverty is virtually nonexistent. See World Bank, 1997e, where it is stated that "urban poverty is negligible" (p. 4) and "Even in 1981 just 0.3 per cent of the urban population lived in absolute poverty" (p. 11). The latter statement is evidently an error, as the Bank's estimates show the urban poverty rate to have been 1.9% in 1981, falling to 0.3% in 1984.

9. See, for example, World Bank, 1992b, p. 5.

10. The relation between food intake and survival is a complex one, depending on many factors, such as climate, temperature, height, weight, level of activity, health status, etc. Individuals vary in the efficiency with which nutrients are utilized by the body. The body may also be able to adapt metabolically to changes in food availability. See Sukhatme, 1982, and Srinivasan, 1981. The substantial debate over these issues is summarized in Dreze and Sen, 1989, pp. 37–42.

11. These problems have been widely observed in other countries as well. For example, see Behrman and Deolalikar, 1987. In China, the difficulties seem to have been compounded by the incompleteness of food consumption data and the aggregated form in which the data are available.

12. See the Appendix to this chapter for a detailed explanation of the derivation of the poverty thresholds.

13. The derivation of the urban poverty threshold is described in detail in the Appendix to this chapter.

14. A "constraint" on consumer preference is a pattern of living that commits consumers to a higher unit cost of food. An example is the form of work organization that compels an individual to receive a higher proportion of food energy from food purchased in prepared form (as distinct from home-cooked food). This is far more widely prevalent in urban China than in rural China.

15. The rural poverty threshold used by the SSB is 236 yuan for 1988 and 540 yuan for 1995, implying a deflator of 228.8 between those years. The SSB's poverty threshold is based on a normative bundle of food providing 2,393 kilocalories per capita per day valued at the weighted average of "planned" and market prices (only market prices since 1990), which is assumed to be 60% of total expenditure of an average household at poverty threshold. The lower SSB poverty threshold, in spite of a higher level of food energy than ours, may appear puzzling. It is due principally to the assumption that 88.4% of kilocalories in the SSB's normative food bundle for the poor is supplied by grain, whereas the SSB's own survey (which is the basis for our composition of food) shows that it is just over 70%. Grain remains a far cheaper source of food energy than the average for the remaining sources, even after the upward adjustment in food prices.

16. Note that for 1988, estimates for overall rural China include households from an additional nine provinces that are not shown in the table because they were not included in the 1995 survey.

17. This is based on the unadjusted CPI.

18. This is estimated by simulating the head count ratio of poverty by combining the Lorenz distribution fitted to the decile group shares of income in 1988 with per capita income of 1995 at 1988 prices and the 1988 poverty threshold (which is the same as the 1995 poverty threshold at 1988 prices).

19. This correlation is for poverty estimates based on the broad poverty threshold without any adjustment in the CPI.

20. To remind the reader, the benchmark year for the estimation of poverty thresholds is 1995. The CPI is used to deflate them to derive poverty thresholds for 1988. That is the reason why adjustments in CPI result in a second set of poverty thresholds for 1988 rather than for 1995.

21. The estimates presented in Table 4.1 correspond to "deep poverty," as shown in Table 4.10. While there is no figure in Table 4.1 for 1988, the estimate for 1989 is 7.42%, well above the 4.1% for 1988 shown in Table 4.10. For 1995 the difference is not as great: 5.9% (1994) in Table 4.1, compared with 4.1% in Table 4.10.

22. Khan, 1996, which does not have an estimate for 1995, shows a reduction of 15% in the Head Count index of rural poverty between 1988 and 1994.

23. See World Bank, 1996, pp. 4, 6, and World Bank, 1997c, p. 11.

24. Xian Zude and Sheng Laiyun, *The Measurement and Decomposition of Rural Poverty of China* (forthcoming), quoted in Zhu Ling, 1997. This is to be distinguished from the official SSB estimates to which reference has been made in section 1.

25. Ren and Chen, 1996, show the following head count ratios:

1991	5.8%	1994	5.7%
1992	4.5%	1995	4.4%
1993	5.1%		

The absence of an estimate for 1988 makes it impossible to compare their trend with ours.

26. It may be noted that the official SSB estimates also show a decline in the Head Count index of rural poverty between 1988 and 1995, although their poverty thresholds do not use an understated CPI. In the absence of information on their method of estimates, it is impossible to guess what this outcome is due to.

27. The Ren and Chen study uses a poverty threshold of 752 yuan for 1991 and 1,547 yuan for 1995, implying a rise in CPI for the poor of 106% over the period. The official urban CPI increased by 84% over the same period. It is unlikely that the understatement of the official CPI was of the order of the difference between the two indices.

Chapter 5

1. See, for instance, UNDP, 1997.

2. Income is measured by a purchasing power parity (PPP) estimate of real GDP per capita. Longevity is life expectancy at birth. Education is measured by a weighted average of adult literacy rates (two-thirds weight) and combined school enrollment rates at primary, secondary, and tertiary levels (one-third weight). For each variable, the actual value used is the distance traveled from a specific international minimum value toward a specific international maximum value, as a percentage of the entire distance from minimum to maximum. The minimum and maximum values established for each indicator is as follows:

Real GDP per capita ($PPP)	$100 and $40,000
Life expectancy at birth	25 years and 85 years
Adult literacy	0% and 100%
Combined gross enrollment rates	0% and 100%

However, in calculating the formula for HDI, real GDP per capita above the world average in 1994 (PPP$5,835) is discounted increasingly heavily as it rises, to reflect the diminishing marginal utility of income. China's GDP per capita in 1994 of PPP$2,604 was below this threshold and thus not subject to discounting. Among the provinces, only Shanghai's per capita GDP was higher than the 1994 international average, and thus had to be adjusted. See UNDP, 1997, Technical note 2, p. 122.

3. See UNDP 1999a, Chapter 1. The official estimates of provincial GDP per capita were used for this calculation, not the survey estimates reported here.

4. The relevant equation is:

$$DHDI = 0.026 - 0.0184*HDI90 + 0.341*DGDPI; \text{ Adjusted } R^2 = 0.977$$
$$(3.12)\quad(-1.24)\qquad\qquad(32.32)$$

where DHDI is difference in HDI value between 1990 and 1995, HDI90 is the 1990 value of HDI, and DGDPI is change in GDP index between 1990 and 1995. This equation explains almost 98% of the variation in growth of HDI between the two dates. See UNDP, 1999a.

5. A substantial additional share of GDP is raised by governments at various levels through extra-budgetary means, but these funds are generally not available for redistributive social programs. See Chapter 7 for a fuller discussion of this issue.

6. See the *Human Development Reports* of recent years for details of the construction of these indices.

7. *Beijing Review* 39.22, 27 May–June 1996.

8. Under conditions of equal treatment for both sexes, 105–106 males are born for every 100 females. Males tend to have a higher infant mortality rate, so the ratio evens up after a few years.

9. Ages reported in this survey are somewhat uncertain, because respondents were asked to report them in years, not months. Thus, a newborn infant would be likely to be reported as age one. It is also a traditional practice to assign an age of one at birth. Moreover, the small numbers of observations for individual ages incline us not to put faith in the accuracy of a given ratio or in trends in this ratio over a sequence of ages. What we believe is significant is that ratios for all ages examined are well above the values expected when both sexes are treated equally.

10. This is consistent with our finding of a higher ratio of males to females for ages zero to five than among infants one or below (see Table 5.2); however, the higher ratios could also have been caused by declining male preference.

11. This issue has been enlighteningly discussed by Amartya Sen. (1989, 1990).

12. Official statistics indicate that 98.8% of children between the ages of six and twelve were enrolled in primary schools in 1996 (*Beijing Review* 39.19, 6–12 May 1996). Sample surveys have found somewhat lower rates, but still well above the rates reported here.

13. The term "cadre" refers to a Communist Party member who holds a leadership position in an organization. See Schurmann, 1966, pp. 162ff.

14. See UNDP, 1999a.

15. Laid-off workers are not included among the unemployed in China's statistics.

16. These include women's health and knowledge, immunization levels, access to health services and to clean water, sanitation, and overall health of the child's environment. See UNICEF, 1989, cited in World Bank, 1997d.

17. See World Bank, 1997d, pp. 12–13. The finding on stagnation of under-five mortality rates is based on standard international practice of applying estimation techniques to data from censuses and fertility surveys. It is challenged by some Chinese researchers, who cite contradictory death registration data to argue that the mortality rates in question have continued to decline.

18. *China Daily*, 16 July 1996.

19. In a regression of total per capita medical expenditures on household per capita income (RYPC) and dummy variables for employment in state enterprises (STATE) or in TVEs (TVE), the coefficients are all highly significant statistically, but very small, and together they explain less than 3% of the variation in medical expenditures:

RURMEDEX = 42.6 + 0.01RYPC + 25.3 TVE − 27.6 STATE, R2 = 0.027

The negative sign for the coefficient on STATE is probably due to the fact that those working in the state sector get all or most of their medical care free.

20. The coefficients on intercept and per capita income are significant at the 1% level, but that on the sector dummy barely misses significance at the 5% level. Adjusted R^2 is only 0.007.

Chapter 6

1. These growth rates are based on the increase in the official CPI as the deflator of personal income. If the adjusted CPIs are used, the growth rates turn out to be lower.

2. See World Bank, 1997b, for arguments why GDP growth rate might have been overestimated.

3. Agriculture's "terms of trade" is the ratio of the "general purchasing price index of farm products" and "general rural retail price index of industrial products," both shown in SSB, 1997. Very little is known about the method of estimating them and their accuracy in reflecting the relative purchasing power of the sectors.

4. See Riskin, 1987. For the classic discussion of shortages and soft budget constraints in socialist economies, see Kornai, 1980.

5. Some readers might be puzzled by the contrast between the fairly high Gini ratios for land and its very low concentration ratios. The Gini ratios are influenced by various geographic factors, such as climate, quality of terrain, and population density. What the low concentration ratios tell us is that, whatever the reasons for inequality of landholdings, income is not one of them.

6. The present writers are among those who expressed such concern in the past. See, for example, Khan et al., 1993.

7. The reference is to gross value of farming, animal husbandry, fishing and forestry, in comparable prices. See *Statistical Yearbook of China, 1997*, pp. 26–27.

8. See Khan, 1996, for details and for comparative data for the Republic of Korea, a country with far scarcer relative endowment of labor.

9. Data provided by Hu Angang. See UNDP, 1999b, Chap. 4.

10. Some of the growth of employment has been purely nominal, as laid off workers are still considered to be employed. Of course, many urban jobs have gone to migrant workers, whose incomes have risen as a result, but migrant workers are not considered part of the urban population.

11. Note that these figures do not contradict the higher share, reported above, of state and collective enterprises in *formal industries* in 1995. The share given here refers to *all* urban employment in 1996.

12. This estimate is by Hu Angang and is reported in UNDP, 1999b, Chap. 4.

13. For a list of various surveys of population mobility in the 1990s, see Cai Fang, 1997.

14. See Khan, 1996, for evidence for the statements made in this paragraph.

15. This is so because some changes in distribution affecting the poor may not be captured by the Gini ratio. Consider, for example, a redistribution between the bottom decile and the second poorest decile which is exactly offset by an opposite redistribution between the ninth decile and the top decile, so that the Gini ratio is unchanged. If the bottom decile represents the poor, then this redistribution will affect poverty estimates.

16. The adjusted R^2 is 0.60 for the fitted regression POV = 36.89 + 2.36 GROWTH (the coefficient of GROWTH being significant at 1% level), while the adjusted R^2 is 0.63 for the fitted regression POV = 23.21 − 11.93 GROWTH + 0.48 GINI (the coefficient of GROWTH being significant at 1% level while the coefficient of GINI is not significant at 10% level). POV is percent change in head count poverty, GROWTH is the rate of income growth, and GINI is percent change in Gini ratio.

17. The adjusted R^2 is 0.63 for the fitted regression equation POV = −50.95 + 0.46 GINI (the coefficient of GINI being significant at 1% level). The adjusted R^2 falls to 0.60 for the fitted regression equation POV = −82.06 + 8.58 GROWTH + 0.49 GINI. The coefficient of GINI is significant at 1% level. Not only is the coefficient of GROWTH insignificant at any reasonable level of probability, its sign is opposite of what is expected. Note that in these regressions for urban provinces, Beijing was excluded because the rate of reduction in head count poverty index cannot be estimated, owing to the fact that its value for 1988 is zero. Variables have the same meaning as in the case of rural China (see the preceding note).

Chapter 7

1. Information reported in this section has been derived from Riskin et al., 1996, Zhu Ling, 1997, and interviews at the Beijing office of the Leading Group for the Development of Poor Areas.

2. The standard is, however, allowed to vary depending on other characteristics of counties. Thus, for example, a higher cut-off income is used for the ethnic minority areas and old revolutionary base areas.

3. China uses the numerical unit *qianwan*, or 10 million. (*Qian* = 1,000, and *wan* = 10,000, so *qianwan*, the product of the two, is equal to 10 million.) The figure 8 in the 8-7 program is in units of *qianwan*, and thus means 80 million. The "7" stands for the number of years left from the program's inauguration to accomplish the goal by the year 2000.

4. At 1995 prices, this target average income for the poor counties would be approximately 882 yuan. Given that household income according to our survey definition is 46% higher than according to the official definition, this would imply a level of about 1,288 yuan for 1995, about 11% higher than our high poverty threshold.

5. An assessment of the poverty alleviation program can be found in UNDP, 1999a.

6. This is discussed in Riskin et al., 1996.

7. These ratios are at current prices. At constant purchasing power of 1988, using the unadjusted official CPIs, the ratio in 1995 would be 2.39.

8. See Khan et al., 1993, for evidence for other Asian countries.

9. This argument is made by Lin, Cai, and Li, 1997.

10. See World Bank, 1997a and 1997c, and UNDP, 1999a, for discussions of agriculture, food security and the environment.

11. See Kung and Liu, 1997, for the results of an opinion survey on this issue.

12. For instance, urban ownership rates for color televisions, washing machines, and refrigerators were 100%, 89% and 75%, respectively, in 1997, as compared with only 27%, 22% and 8.5% in rural areas. See UNDP, 1999a, Chap. 4.

13. Lin, Cai, and Li, 1997, show that during the reform period, inequality among these three regions has grown while inequality among provinces within each of these three regions has actually diminished.

14. Riskin et al., 1996.

15. World Bank, 1997b, p. 24.

16. China uses a consolidated budget approach, in which the budget at each level includes those of lower levels. The ratios given in this paragraph thus refer to total revenue of both central and local governments, as a percentage of GDP. Data can be found in the *Statistical Yearbook of China* for various years. See also Wong, Heady, and West 1997; UNDP 1999; Wong 1999; World Bank, 1997b.

17. Naughton, 1999.

18. Wong, 1999, p. 1. See also Naughton, 1999, who estimates extrabudgetary funds at about 7% of GDP.

19. Wong, 1999, pp. 6–7.

20. This paragraph is based on Wang Shaoguang, 1999, and UNDP, 1999b.

21. Shanghai, Beijing, and Tianjin are municipalities with provincial status, as is Chongqing since 1997.

22. Politically sensitive Tibet is a conspicuous exception, although we do not have information on the size of its subsidy in 1980–1981.

23. See Wong, Heady, and West, 1997, for a discussion of local finances.

24. Fiscal decentralization was not the only reason for the decline in public spending on health. An important additional cause was that the "cooperative medical system" (CMS), which provided and financed rural health care under the rural communes, collapsed when the communes were dismantled in the early 1980s.

25. Naughton, 1999, argues that the current system provides many incentives for laid off workers to remain associated with their enterprises or to insist on reemployment in the state sector, and that "a credible, adequately funded program of social benefits will in turn make it credible that the government is requiring enterprises and workers to establish a new arms-length relationship." See UNDP, 1999b.

26. See Chapter 6; Hu Angang, 1998; and Brandt and Zhu, 1996.

27. Thus, Gansu reported 21.4% of its rural work force working as hired hands out of the province. Other major source areas are Sichuan, Ningxia, Anhui, Henan, and Jiangxi. See Hu Angang, 1998.

28. According to our estimates, there were 104 million extreme poor, and on the average each has a shortfall of 208 yuan from poverty threshold. This makes the total resources needed to bring all of them out of extreme poverty 21.63 billion yuan. Assuming that the official estimate of 65 million poor is correct, assuming further that the average income gap of the poor is 25% (which is close to the average income gap of different categories of poor according to our estimates), and using the official poverty threshold of 540 yuan for 1995, only 8.8 billion yuan was necessary to eliminate poverty through a perfectly targeted income subsidy program.

29. See *China Daily*, 16 July 1996, p. 2.

30. For discussions of China's environmental situation, see *China Quarterly*, 1998; Smil, 1993; UNDP, 1999a; UNDP, 1999b; *China's Agenda 21*, 1994; and *Environmental Action Plan of China*, 1994.

31. See World Bank, 1999.

Chapter 8

1. Hereafter, all such comparisons refer to 1988 and 1995 unless otherwise specified.

2. Our male/female ratios are all higher even than the official statistics, a result for which we have no explanation. Our sample sizes are small for individual age cohorts, which introduces the possibility of considerable sampling error.

3. See Kung, 1994, 1995.

4. See Kung and Liu, 1997, for the results of an opinion survey on this issue.

5. Land allocations are of two types: subsistence (*kouliang*) fields and contract fields. There is some record of discrimination against women in some places in the allocation of contract land, but subsistence land is usually allocated on a strict per capita basis.

6. Thomas G. Rawski (1999) argues that official statistics greatly underestimate the growth of employment in the non-agricultural economy, especially in construction, transport, and trade; that the formal sector (including state, collective, private, TVE and "other" enterprises) absorbed more than the increment to the labor force between 1990 and 1994/5; and that this picture changed only after 1995. Our argument focuses on urban industry alone.

Bibliography

Allen, R. G. D. 1975. *Index Numbers, Theory and Practice*. London: Macmillan.

Amjad, R., and A. R. Kemal. 1996. "Macro Economic Policies and Their Impact on Poverty Alleviation in Pakistan." Islamabad: Pakistan Institute of Development Economics.

Asian Development Bank. 1993. *Key Indicators of Developing Asian and Pacific Countries*. Manila: Oxford University Press.

Balisacan, Arsenio. 1996. "What Is the Real Story on Poverty in the Philippines? A Re-examination of Evidence and Policy." Ms., School of Economics, University of the Philippines.

Behrman, Jere, and A. Deolalikar. 1987. "Will Developing Country Nutrition Improve with Income? A Case Study of Rural South India." *Journal of Political Economy* 95, no. 3, pp. 492–507.

Brandt, Loren, and Xiaodong Zhu. 1996. "Redistribution in a Decentralizing Economy: Growth and Inflation in Post-Reform China." Ms. University of Toronto, Department of Economics.

Brenner, Mark. 2000. "Re-Examining the Distribution of Wealth in Rural China," Ph.D. dissertation at University of California, Riverside.

Cai, Fang, 1997. "China's Population: Structure, Dynamics and Impact on Economic Development." Background paper for the China National Human Development Report. Beijing: United Nations Development Programme.

Cambodia. 1994. *Socio-Economic Survey of Cambodia, 1993/94*. Phnom Penh: Department of Statistics, Ministry of Planning.

China Quarterly. 1998. Number 156 (December), Special Issue on China's Environment.

China's Agenda 21. 1994. *Zhongguo 21 shiji yicheng, Zhongguo 21 shiji renkou, huanjing yu fazhan baipishu* [*China's Agenda 21, White Paper on China's*

175

Population, Environment and Development in the 21st Century]. Beijing: China Environmental Sciences Press.

Dreze, Jean, and Amartya Sen. 1989. *Hunger and Public Action*. Oxford: Clarendon Press.

Environmental Action Plan of China, 1991–2000. 1994. Produced by National Environmental Protection Agency and the State Planning Commission of the People's Republic of China. Beijing: China Environmental Science Press.

Fei, John C. H., Gustav Ranis, and S. W. Y. Kuo. 1978. "Growth and the Family Distribution of Income by Factor Components." *Quarterly Journal of Economics*, pp. 17–53.

Fields, Gary S. 1980. *Poverty, Inequality and Development*. Cambridge: Cambridge University Press.

Griffin, Keith, and Zhao Renwei, eds. 1993. *The Distribution of Income in China*. London: Macmillan.

Guonwuyuan Yanjiushi Ketizu (Study Group of State Planning Commission Research Office). 1997. "Guanyu Chengzhen Jumin Geren Shouru Chajude Fenxi He Jianyi" ["An Analysis and Proposal Concerning Income Inequality Among Urban Residents"]. *Jingji Yanjiu* no. 8 (August 1997): pp. 3–10.

Hu Angang. 1998. "No. 6 National Conditions Report: Employment and Development: China's Employment Problem and Employment Strategy." Ms., National Conditions Analysis and Study Group, Chinese Academy of Sciences.

Hu Shanlian. 1997. "Health and Nutrition: Background Paper for the China National Human Development Report." Ms. UNDP, Beijing.

Jalan, Jyotsna, and Martin Ravallion. 1997. "Are There Dynamic Gains from a Poor-Area Development Program?" *Journal of Public Economics* 67, no. 1, pp. 65–85.

Jalan, Jyotsna, and Martin Ravallion. 1998. "Transient Poverty in Postreform Rural China." *Journal of Comparative Economics* 26, pp. 338–357.

Kakwani, Nanak. 1980. *Income Inequality and Poverty: Methods of Estimation and Policy Applications*. Oxford: Oxford University Press.

Kakwani, Nanak. 1986. *Analyzing Redistribution Policies: A Study Using Australian Data*. Cambridge: Cambridge University Press.

Khan, A. R. 1996. *The Impact of Recent Macroeconomic and Sectoral Changes on the Poor and Women in China*. New Delhi: International Labour Organization, South Asia Multidisciplinary Advisory Team (ILO/SAAT).

Khan, A. R., K. Griffin, C. Riskin, and Zhao Renwei. 1992. "Household Income and its Distribution in China." *China Quarterly*, no. 132 (December), pp. 1086–1100.

Khan, A. R., K. Griffin, C. Riskin, and Zhao Renwei. 1993. "Household Income and its Distribution in China." In Keith Griffin and Zhao Renwei (eds.), *The Distribution of Income in China*. London: Macmillan, pp. 25–73.

Kornai, Janos, 1980. *Economics of Shortage*. Amsterdam: North Holland.

Kung, J. K. 1994. "Egalitarianism, Subsistence Provision and Work Incentives in China's Agricultural Collectives." *World Development* 22, no. 2, pp. 175–187.

Kung, J. K. 1995. "Equal Entitlement versus Tenure Security under a Regime of Collective Property Rights." *Journal of Comparative Economics* 21, no. 2, pp. 82–111.

Kung, J. K., and Liu Shouying. 1997. "Farmers' Preferences Regarding Ownership and Land Tenure in Post-Mao China: Unexpected Evidence from Eight Counties." *China Journal* 38, pp. 33–63.

Kuo, S. W. Y., Gustav Ranis, and John C. H. Fei. 1981. *Rapid Growth with Improved Distribution in the Republic of China, 1952–79*. Boulder, Colo.: Westview.

Li Shi. 2000. "Labor Migration and Income Distribution in Rural China." in Riskin, Zhao and Li, 2000.

Lin, Justin, Fang Cai, and Zhou Li. 1997. *Social Consequences of Economic Reform in China: An Analysis of Regional Disparity in the Transition Period*. Ms., report for United Nations Development Programme, Beijing.

Lyons, Thomas P. 1994. *Poverty and Growth in a South China County: Anxi, Fujian, 1949–1992*. Ithaca, N.Y.: Cornell University Press.

Naughton, Barry. 1995. *Growing Out of the Plan: Chinese Economic Reform, 1978–1993*. Cambridge: Cambridge University Press.

Naughton, Barry. 1999. "Human Development and the Role of the State in China: Background Paper Prepared for the 1999 China Human Development Report." Ms. UNDP, Beijing.

Park, Albert, and Scott Rozelle, eds. 1994. *Promoting Economic Development in China's Poor Areas*. Research policy briefs presented by members of the China Poverty Research Association at a discussion forum sponsored by the Ford Foundation, Beijing.

Park, Albert, S. Rozelle, C. Wong, and C. Ren, 1996, "Distributional Consequences of Reforming Local Public Finance in China." *China Quarterly*, no. 147 (September): 751–778.

Piazza, Alan, and Echo H. Liang. "The State of Poverty in China: Its Causes and Remedies." Paper presented to conference on "Unintended Consequences of China's Economic Reforms." Harvard University, 23–24 May 1997.

Ravallion, Martin, and Shaohua Chen. 1998. "When Economic Reform Is Faster than Statistical Reform: Measuring and Explaining Inequality in Rural China." Policy Research Working Paper 1902, World Bank Development Research Group, Washington, D.C.

Rawski, Thomas G. 1999. "China: Prospects for Full Employment." Employment and Training Papers, no. 47, International Labour Office, Geneva.

Ren Caifang and Chen Xiaojie. 1996. "Size, Situation and Trend of Poverty in Urban China." *Research Reference*, No. 65, Beijing.

Riskin, Carl. 1987. *China's Political Economy: The Quest for Development since 1949*. New York: Oxford University Press.

Riskin, Carl. 1993. "Income Distribution and Poverty in Rural China." In Griffin and Zhao, pp. 135–170.

Riskin, Carl, et al. 1996. *Rural Poverty Alleviation in China: An Assessment and Recommendations*, report prepared for the United Nations Development Programme, Beijing.

Riskin, Carl, Zhao Renwei, and Li Shi, eds. 2000. *China's Retreat from Equality: Income Distribution and Economic Transition*. Armonk, N.Y.: M. E. Sharpe.

Rozelle, Scott, A. Park, V. Benziger, and C. Ren. 1997. "Helping Households or Subsidizing the State: Assessing the Record of China's Poor Area Policies." Paper presented at conference, "Unintended Social Consequences of Chinese Economic Reforms," Harvard University, 23–24 May 1997.

Schurmann, Franz. 1966. *Ideology and Organization in Communist China*. Berkeley: University of California Press.

Sen, Amartya. 1989. "Women's Survival as a Development Problem." *Bulletin of the American Academy of Arts and Sciences*, 43.2, pp. 14–29.

Sen, Amartya. 1990. "More than 100 Million Women are Missing." *New York Review of Books* 37, no. 20, pp. 61–66.

Sen, Amartya. 1997. *On Economic Inequality*. Oxford: Oxford University Press.

Smil, Vaclav. 1993. *China's Environmental Crisis*. Armonk, N.Y.: M. E. Sharpe.

Song, Lina. 1998. *Gender Effects on Household Resource Allocation in Rural China*. Oxford: Institute of Economics and Statistics.

Srinivasan, T. N. 1981. "Malnutrition: Some Measurement and Policy Issues." *Journal of Development Economics* 8, pp. 3–19.

State Statistical Bureau (SSB). 1989. *China Statistical Yearbook 1989*. Beijing: China Statistical Publishing House.

State Statistical Bureau (SSB). 1995. *China Statistical Yearbook 1995*. Beijing: China Statistical Publishing House.

State Statistical Bureau (SSB). 1996. *China Statistical Yearbook 1996*. Beijing: China Statistical Publishing House.

State Statistical Bureau (SSB). 1997. *China Statistical Yearbook 1997*. Beijing: China Statistical Publishing House.

Sukhatme, P. V. 1982. "Measurement of Undernutrition." *Economic and Political Weekly 17*, no. 50, pp. 2000–2016.

United Nations Children's Fund (UNICEF). 1989. *The State of the World's Children*. Oxford: Oxford University Press.

United Nations Children's Fund (UNICEF). 1995. *Children and Women of China: A Situation Analysis* (draft). Beijing: UNICEF.

United Nations Development Programme (UNDP). 1997. *Human Development Report 1997*. New York: Oxford University Press.

United Nations Development Programme (UNDP). 1999a. *China Human Development Report*. New York: Oxford University Press.

United Nations Development Programme (UNDP). 1999b. *China Human Development Report 1999*. Beijing: UNDP.

Wang Shaoguang. 1999. "The Changing Role of Government." Background paper prepared for *China Human Development Report, 1999*. Ms., UNDP, Beijing.

Wong, Christine. 1999. "Converting Fees into Taxes: Reform of Extrabudgetary Funds and Intergovernmental Fiscal Relations in China, 1999 and Beyond." Paper presented at annual meetings of American Economic Association, New York, January 1999.

Wong, Christine, C. Heady, and L. West. 1997. *Financing Local Development in the People's Republic of China*. Oxford: Oxford University Press.

World Bank. 1990a. *China: Macroeconomic Stability and Industrial Growth under Decentralized Socialism*. Washington, D.C.

World Bank. 1990b. *China: Revenue Mobilization and Tax Policy*. Washington, D.C.

World Bank. 1992a. *China: Reform and the Role of the Plan in the 1990s*. Washington, D.C.

World Bank. 1992b. *China: Strategies for Reducing Poverty in the 1990s*. Washington, D.C.

World Bank. 1995a. *World Tables, 1995*. Baltimore and London: Johns Hopkins University Press.

World Bank. 1995b. *China: Macroeconomic Stability in a Decentralized Economy*. Washington, D.C.

World Bank. 1996. "Poverty in China: What Do The Numbers Say?" Background Note, East Asia and Pacific Region. Washington, D.C.

World Bank. 1997a. *At China's Table: Food Security Options*. Washington, D.C.

World Bank 1997b. *China 2020: Development Challenges in The New Century*. Washington, D.C.

World Bank. 1997c. *Clear Water, Blue Skies: China's Environment in the New Century*. Washington, D.C.

World Bank. 1997d. *Financing Health Care: Issues and Options for China*. Washington, D.C.

World Bank. 1997e. *Sharing Rising Incomes: Disparities in China*. Washington, D.C.

World Bank. 1997f. *World Development Indicators 1997*. Washington, D.C.

World Bank. 1998. *World Development Indicators 1998*. Washington, D.C.

World Bank. 1999. *Global Economic Prospects and the Developing Countries 1998/99*. Washington, D.C.

Zhu Ling. 1997. "Poverty and Poverty Alleviation in China." Background paper for *China Human Development Report 1997*. Ms. Beijing: United Nations Development Programme.

Index

agriculture, 4, 6, 108
  decline in growth, 125–26
  feminization of, 89
  income, 35, 161n.3
  resources for, 126–27
  terms of trade, 5, 105, 106, 126, 154–55, 165n.19, 170n.3
  See also land distribution
Anhui province, 48, 65–69, 71, 72, 74, 75, 83, 84, 117–19

Beijing, 48, 65–68, 71, 72, 74, 83, 84, 117–20
broad poverty, 66–69, 71, 73–74, 119, 134, 147, 156
budget, 172n.16

Cambodia, 78
Chen Xiaojie, 77, 78
China National Human Development Report, 82
CMS. *See* Cooperative Medical System
coastal development strategy, 144
coastal provinces, 49, 155, 165n.22
  See also specific provinces
concentration ratio, 108, 161–62n.6, 164n.7, 164n.11, 170n.5
consumer price index (CPI), 18–19, 78, 161n.5
  differences between rural and urban, 45
  indicators of change, 19

and poverty estimates, 56, 75–76, 147
  for poverty thresholds, 62–64, 166n.7, 168n.27
  and reduction in rural poverty, 75, 76
  rural poverty estimates based on adjusted, 70
  urban poverty estimates based on adjusted, 72–73
Cooperative Medical System (CMS), 96, 173n.24
CPI. *See* consumer price index

debt, 5
decentralization, 129–33, 153, 156, 173n.24
deep poverty, 69, 71, 74–75

economic growth
  and decline in poverty reduction, 117–20
  impact on human development, 81–85
  and income distribution, 7–8, 144
  in period of reform, 3–4, 143
education, 82, 87–88, 92, 93, 168n.2
efficiency, 6
employment. *See* labor; unemployment
Engel function, 58
entrepreneurship, 18, 37

181

equality, 7–8
    See also income distribution,
        inequality
exports, 4–5, 6
extra-budgetary funds, 130–31, 153
extreme poverty, 69–70, 72, 75,
    134, 147, 156, 173n.28

farming. *See* agriculture
FDI. *See* foreign direct investment
fiscal system, 129–35, 156–57
food energy consumption, 58–59,
    64, 78, 166n.10, 167n.14
foreign capital, 5, 7
foreign direct investment (FDI), 5,
    6, 7, 107, 144
foreign trade, 5–6, 144
Fujian province, 86

Gansu province, 48, 65–68, 71, 72,
    74, 83, 84, 86, 118, 119
GDP. *See* gross domestic product
gender issues, 85–95, 149–50
    access to education, 87–88
    sex ratios and male preference, 86–
        87
    treatment of girls within
        household, 88
    women in labor force, 85–86, 88–
        95, 149
Gini ratio for income, 161–62n.6,
    171n.15
    as index of inequality, 28–29
    international comparison of, 164–
        65n.16
    overall for China, 40, 41, 43,
        115
    provincial, 47–49, 117, 119–20
    for rural income, 30, 144–45
    standard error, 163n.4
    for urban income, 36–37, 134,
        135, 156
    See also concentration ratio
Gini ratio for land, 108, 170n.5
globalization, 4–7, 110, 141, 143,
    144
GNP. *See* gross national product
great leap forward (1958–1960),
    106
gross domestic product (GDP), 3
    decentralization in public finance
        relative to, 153
    gap between growth and increase
        in personal income, 104–7, 151

growth between 1988 and 1995,
    103, 117
    and human development, 82–85,
        102
    purchasing power parity estimate,
        168n.2
    ratio of fiscal surplus, 132
gross national product (GNP), 25–26
    gap between growth and increase
        in personal income, 26–27
    level and growth of, 25–26
Guangdong province, 48, 65–69,
    71, 72, 74, 83, 84, 118–20
Guangxi province, 86
Guizhou province, 48, 65, 66, 67,
    68, 118

HDI. *See* Human Development
    Index
Head-Count index of poverty, 53,
    54, 66, 69, 71–77, 165n.3,
    168n.26
health care, 95–101, 150
Hebei province, 48, 65–69, 117,
    118, 123
Henan province, 48, 65–68, 71, 72,
    74, 83, 84, 117–19
household income, 14–27, 107,
    163n.16
housing income, 15, 16, 18–22, 35,
    40, 145, 160n.1, 164n.11
Hubei province, 48, 65–68, 71, 72,
    74, 83, 84, 118, 119
human development, 82–85, 148–50
    gender issues, 85–95, 149–50
    health care issues, 95–101, 150
Human Development Index (HDI),
    81–85, 102, 148, 168n.2
Human Development Report, 82
Hunan province, 46, 48, 65–68,
    118

income
    components of rural, 14–15, 144–
        45
    components of urban, 16, 145–46
    definitions of, 14, 22–25
    and human development, 82–85
    levels and changes, 17–22
    personal, 104–7, 151
    See also income distribution
income distribution, 9–12
    change from 1988 to 1995, 43–
        44, 50, 143, 144, 146, 151

and economic growth, 7–8, 144
evolution of inequality, 28–51
interprovincial inequality, 45–47
intraprovincial inequality, 47–49
overall in China, 40–44, 51, 146
policies for reduction of
   inequality, 121–42, 154
regional inequality, 44–50, 116–
   17, 128–29, 155–56
rural, 17–20, 29–35, 43–45, 50,
   107–9, 115, 118, 125–28
sources of increased inequality,
   107–17
urban, 20–22, 35–40, 44–45, 50,
   115, 118, 119, 125–28
industrialization, 110, 152
infant mortality, 86, 95, 100
investment, 26, 105–7, 151, 158

Jiangsu province, 48, 65–68, 71, 72,
   74, 83, 84, 118, 119
Jiangxi province, 48, 65–68, 86,
   118
Jilin province, 48, 65–68, 117, 118
jobs. See labor; unemployment

kilocalories, 78–79

labor, 6, 174n.6
   migrant, 138, 171n.10
   output elasticity of employment,
      110–12, 137, 153
   second jobs, 92, 94
   social protection, 6–7
   urban employment, 135–36
   women's issues, 85–86, 88–95,
      149
   See also unemployment; wages
land distribution, 107–9, 127, 151–
   52, 170n.5, 174n.5
Laspeyre index, 161n.5
Liaoning province, 48, 65–69, 71,
   72, 74, 83, 84, 118–20
life expectancy, 95, 168n.2
Li Peng, 126
Li Shi, 82
literacy, 92, 168n.2
longevity, 82, 168n.2
Lorenz curves, 34, 38, 117, 163n.2
low-income countries, 159n.6

macroeconomic policies, 140–41
male preference, 86–87
Mao Zedong, 143

medical care. See health care
middle-income countries, 159n.6
migrant labor, 138, 171n.10
migration, 11–12, 61, 115–16, 137–
   39, 155, 157, 160n.17

National 8–7 Plan for Poverty
   Reduction, 122, 123, 124
nutrition, 58–59, 60, 64

over-accumulation, 106

Paasche index, 18–19, 161nn.4–5
per capita income, 162n.8
per capita income available for
   living, 162n.8
population mobility. See migration
poverty, 6, 8, 52–80, 146–48
   consumer price indices for
      thresholds, 62–64
   correlation with urban
      unemployment, 112–14
   decline in reduction, 103–20, 143,
      144, 151
   deriving thresholds, 78–80
   estimates of, 57–62, 64–75
   evidence on trends, 52–56
   limitations of existing estimates,
      56
   policies for reduction of, 121–42,
      154–57
   rural, 54, 65–70, 75, 76, 78–79,
      147, 148, 154–57, 166n.6,
      167n.15
   urban, 55, 70–76, 79–80, 166n.8
private enterprise, 7, 37
property income, 18, 21
   See also housing income
Proportionate Poverty Gap index,
   53, 54, 64–67, 71–72, 165n.3
public finance, 115, 131, 153
public resources, 155
purchasing power parity, 168n.2

Qinghai province, 82

ration coupons, 164n.10
Ren Caifang, 77, 78
retirement income, 21, 22
rural economy, 4, 54, 65–70, 128,
   154–55
rural income
   components of, 14–15, 144–45
   distribution of, 29–35, 43–45, 50

rural income (*continued*)
  and distribution of land, 107–9
  inequality with urban, 28–40,
    115, 125–28, 146
  levels and changes, 17–20
  rate of growth, 118
  real rate of increase in, 22–23
  wages, 14, 16, 17, 19, 23, 30, 34,
    50, 109, 144, 152
rural population, 164n.14
rural poverty, 54, 65–70, 75–79,
    147, 148, 154–57, 166n.6,
    167n.15

savings, 7, 140
sex ratios, 86–87
Shaanxi province, 48, 65–68, 118
Shandong province, 48, 65–68, 118
Shanghai province, 132
Shanxi province, 48, 65–68, 71, 72,
    74, 83, 84, 118, 119
Sheng Laiyun, 77
Sichuan province, 48, 65–68, 71,
    72, 118
SOEs. *See* state-owned enterprises
special economic zones, 6
SSB. *See* State Statistical Bureau
state-household fiscal interaction,
    133–35
state-owned enterprises (SOEs), 130
State Statistical Bureau (SSB), 8–11,
    22–25, 56, 146, 159n.2,
    162n.8, 162n.11
subsidies, 105, 115, 134, 145, 156
sustainable human development, 81

targeted income subsidy approach,
    139–40
tariffs, 5
taxes, 34, 105, 115, 134, 145, 156
Theil index, 163n.1
township and village enterprises
    (TVEs), 84, 128, 133
trade. *See* exports; foreign trade
transfer payments, 129–35

trickle-down approach, 157
TVEs. *See* township and village
    enterprises

UNDP. *See* United Nations
    Development Programme
unemployment, 107
  concealed, 153, 157
  registered, 112–13
  urban, 112–14, 135–36, 147–48
  women's, 94–95, 149
United Nations Development
    Programme (UNDP), 81, 82
urban income
  components of, 16, 145–46
  distribution of, 35–40, 44–45, 50
  estimates of, 23–24
  inequality with rural, 28–40, 115,
    118, 119, 125–28, 146
  levels and changes, 20–22
  per capita disposable, 20
  rate of growth, 25, 118
  wages, 20, 36, 39, 50, 110–14
urban poverty, 70–76, 79–80,
    166n.8

wages, 162n.11
  rural income, 14, 16, 17, 19, 23,
    30, 34, 50, 109, 144, 145,
    152
  urban income, 20, 36, 39, 50,
    110–14, 145
  women's, 89, 91, 93
Weighted Poverty Gap index, 53,
    54, 64–67, 71–72, 166n.3
women. *See* gender issues
work. *See* labor
World Bank, 8, 76–77, 146, 166n.8

Xian Zude, 77

Yunnan province, 48, 65–68, 71,
    72, 74, 75, 83, 84, 118, 119

Zhejiang province, 48, 65–68, 118

DATE D